THE 8<small>TH</small> FIELD
HOSPITAL

ANDREW C. CARR, M.D.

Note for Librarians: a cataloguing record for this book that includes
Dewey Decimal Classification and US Library of Congress numbers
is available from the Library and Archives of Canada. The complete
cataloguing record can be obtained from their online database at:
www.collectionscanada.ca/amicus/index-e.html
ISBN 1-4120-5718-3
Printed in Victoria, BC, Canada

Gratitude to my two copy editors:
Carol Kirsch & Carol Dukes
Photography by Dr. Andrew C. Carr
For information, please contact:
Dr. Andrew C. Carr
acrrcarr@yahoo.com
To learn more about the medical patients who Dr. Carr saw during
his Vietnam tour of duty, please see an article entitled, "Neurology
in the Vietnam War: Captain Carr's Patients. Military Medicine,
169, 10:768, 2004.

TRAFFORD

Offices in Canada, USA, Ireland, UK and Spain
This book was published *on-demand* in cooperation with Trafford
Publishing. On-demand publishing is a unique process and service
of making a book available for retail sale to the public taking
advantage of on-demand manufacturing and Internet marketing.
On-demand publishing includes promotions, retail sales,
manufacturing, order fulfilment, accounting and collecting royalties
on behalf of the author.
Book sales for North America and international:
Trafford Publishing, 6E–2333 Government St.,
Victoria, BC v8t 4p4 CANADA
phone 250 383 6864 (toll-free 1 888 232 4444)
fax 250 383 6804; email to orders@trafford.com
Book sales in Europe:
Trafford Publishing (uk) Ltd., Enterprise House, Wistaston Road
Business Centre, Wistaston Road, Crewe, Cheshire cw2 7rp
UNITED KINGDOM
phone 01270 251 396 (local rate 0845 230 9601)
facsimile 01270 254 983; orders.uk@trafford.com
Order online at:
www.trafford.com/robots/05-0616.html

10 9 8 7 6 5 4 3

This book is dedicated to my wife, Roberta, who typed the pages from my dictation. She kept after me to finish the book while I could still remember my stories.

It is also dedicated to my grandchildren, Patrick and Nicholas, so they can see another side of their Papa Andy.

Lastly, it is dedicated to my daughter, Christina, who was young, but probably still remembers the time when her dad was away serving his country.

Dear Keith,
I know this doctor author
from Kaiser Bellflower.
Thought you might enjoy
his memory of Vietnam.
Jean
Happy Birthday!

AUTHOR'S NOTE

*O*ne talks about the fog of war, clouding how things actually happened. In my case this may be the mist of memory because I am writing these stories 38 years after the events occurred. I find that even after so many years, these stories are still quite vivid for me. Pictures I took while serving in Vietnam reinforce the accuracy of the stories that are depicted in this book. If I captured a memory differently from how others would remember it, it was not intentional.

In the beginning, I recorded my observations of life in Vietnam in a journal, but when my commanding officer saw what I was doing, he told me to destroy the journal. I learned that there is a policy against keeping a journal in a combat zone. The Army feared that the enemy could capture it and learn strategic military information such as troop strength, deployment and other secrets. My journal would have disappointed the enemy because it contained no classified information. It was destroyed nonetheless, and I did not keep another written journal from that point forward.

Contents

THE BEGINNING

*M*y high school years were filled with news of the Korean War. Students from my high school were required to register for the draft and most boys were drafted after they graduated. If one managed to get into college, however, he obtained what was called a "college deferment." In an effort to have superior prospective students get into college before they were drafted, the Ford Foundation set up a special scholarship that would take students from their junior year in high school and put them directly into college. My friend, David Ashley, obtained such a scholarship; my grades were not high enough for me to qualify for it. David skipped his fourth year of high school and went directly to Yale University; but he did come back to participate in graduation activities with his friends and classmates.

After high school I was accepted into college, thus becoming exempt from the draft. After my first year in college it became apparent to the government that many students were in bogus colleges that had sprung up for the sole purpose of helping young men evade the draft. Rather than challenging the credentials of the colleges, the government decided to set up a universal test for all male college students. This test was supposedly designed to separate serious college students from those who were using their college status as a means to avoid the draft. It was an extremely difficult test-at least for me. In order to retain my college exempt status, I had to get an 80% on the test. I obtained an 86%, two points higher than my brother Irvin's score. To my knowledge, that was the only time I ever bested him in an academic achievement.

I got through college immune from the draft. By the time I matriculated, young men were no longer being drafted for the Korean

War. When I went to medical school, no one was taking precautions to exempt themselves from the draft as there was no war at the time and none appeared to be looming. There was a program called the Berry Plan that stated you could be exempted from the draft during four years in a medical school, but you had to pay back those years by joining the Army upon completion of medical school. Few students took advantage of this plan although it was popular the previous four years. I completed medical school, internship, and residency without thinking more about the draft.

In the later part of my residency, the Vietnam War was starting to heat up. Following my residency, I was doing a fellowship in pediatric neurology when I received my greetings from Uncle Sam stating that I had been drafted. I learned that physicians could be drafted up to the age of 35.

I was scheduled for my pre-induction physical examination at the Boston Naval yard. At the induction center, I saw a great number of my fellow medical school colleagues. The physical exam at the center was like no other physical exam I had ever taken. We were all lined up in huge rooms—nearly naked—and indifferent physicians checked us over briefly. I was taken to a large room to provide a urine sample. We were watched over closely by Army personnel to make sure we did not add sugar or some other chemical substance to our urine that would cause us to be rejected by the military.

Next came a vision exam where opticians found that the vision in my left eye could not be corrected better than 20/70. This fact should have precluded me from being on active duty. However, I was told that as a physician, and doing physician work, my vision was not as important as someone who would be in active combat. My results were changed to 20/30, which was acceptable to the Army.

A hearing exam came next and it was discovered that I had high tone hearing loss. This condition was attributed to me not wearing ear protection during my skeet shooting adventures as a youth. Again, I was told that this condition disqualified me from serving in combat areas, but, as a physician, I did not need perfect hearing like soldiers in combat did. My hearing exam was reported as normal, and with that I was told I passed my pre-induction physical with flying colors.

When I asked how long it usually took from the time of having the physical and having to report for duty, I was told it was usually more than six months. That news made me happy; now I could finish my pediatric fellowship. I felt uneasy about being drafted, but I was relieved that I would be finishing this final phase of my formal medical education.

The next bit of information I received from the Army was a lot of paperwork including forms asking where I would like to be stationed. My wife and I agonized over these forms for hours. After much thought, we decided it would be nice to experience Germany as our number one choice. Hawaii made the number two spot on our short list, and we concluded with Florida as our third option. We actually felt a bit of excitement as we pondered these potential new homes. We could almost hear our young daughter, Christina, say her first German words.

Two weeks later, at midnight, my telephone rang and upon answering it, I received an audio telegram from the Army. The telegram consisted mostly of numbers. I later found out that these were routing numbers which defined financial responsibility to various bases, etc. Hidden in the text of this huge telegram I detected the words "report to Fort Sam Houston February 4, 1966." Noting that this date was four days away, I asked the operator to please reread that part to me. She said she was going off duty and she didn't have the time, but that I would get the full telegram the next day. I had an uneasy and sleepless night.

When I reread the telegram in the morning, it confirmed that I did indeed have to report in four days to Fort Sam Houston. The telegram was generated from Fort Mead in Maryland and it had a major's signature with a telephone number. I immediately called the major and told him I was a physician, I had patient responsibilities, I had a family, and I had not yet made out my preference for station locations. He said that being a physician did not matter because all of his notices were sent to physicians. He said not to worry about the assignment of areas because a spot had already been selected for me. "But I have to make arrangements for my family to go with me," I anxiously replied. His response, "You do not need to worry about your family because where you are going families are not allowed to go," sent chills down my spine.

I inquired about those destinations that would meet this criterion. He replied with little emotion, "I can't tell you, but there are only two places that families are not allowed to go. One is to Korea and the other is to Vietnam. And it doesn't appear that you are going to Korea." Stunned and expressing my disbelief, I said, "But the timing is only four days away. I have so much to take care of before I can leave."

After a brief pause, he acknowledged my hardship and said I could have six days, but I would have to report immediately with no other extensions. He told me that this was the best he could do as the Army was trying to fit in a whole class of physician indoctrination between the regular scheduled classes. By giving me two extra days, he told me I would miss the courses in military courtesy but he thought I could figure that out on my own. So, with no other recourse, I traveled in the middle of winter to Fort Sam Houston for my Army indoctrination. In retrospect, I found that missing those two first training days on military courtesy would later come back to haunt me.

MY MARCHING ORDERS

*I*n most cases when a person is assigned Army duty, he or she receives a packet of orders. Normally there are 30 or 40 duplicate orders that have specific numbers on them. These orders are distributed during various phases of the induction process. I did not get the duplicate orders because of the urgency with which my class was assembled; a single telegram was all that I had available. When I arrived at Fort Sam Houston, I showed my telegram to the appropriate person and was assured that arrangements would be made at each step of the way without the duplicate orders one normally receives.

I was amazed at the power of this one piece of paper. For example, upon arriving at Fort Sam Houston there was no room for me in the usual Bachelor Officer Quarters (BOQ), so I was housed in a nearby motel. All I had to do was show the housing officer my telegram and the room was automatically paid for.

When I arrived at the motel, the desk clerk asked if I wanted to join "the club." Having no idea what he was talking about, I asked, "What club?" He repeated the words "the club" as if I should know what they meant. My quizzical look clued him to tell me that San Antonio was a dry town. I told him I had just passed the bar on my way to register at the motel. "No," he replied. "You just passed 'the club.'" It appeared that all the motels had a private club where alcoholic beverages could be served. It was legal to serve alcohol in a private club, but illegal to operate a bar. I asked how much it would cost to join "the club." The clerk replied, "Nothing. Just fill out this membership form and show your card when you order a drink." It was strange to me to be in a dry town where people would go to restaurants and bring their own liquor in a brown paper bag, and, then have to pay a $5 or $6 "set-up" fee. It was also strange to live in a dry town where it was not illegal to drive with open containers in your car. That was my first introduction to San Antonio, Texas.

I returned to my room and as soon as I unpacked, I received notification to report to the medical field service school at 0800 hours the next morning. I was told that a jeep would be sent for me at 0730 hours. I asked what 0730 hours meant in "real" time. When I inquired about why the Army did not use a normal 12-hour clock to report time, I was told that it is more accurate to use a 24 hour clock since no A.M. or P.M. designation was required. For me it got a little complicated in the afternoon until I got use to the new "military time."

The next morning I arrived at the field medical school to start my Army training. The first few days we learned about tactics and military terminology. I later learned that the tactics they taught us were basically World War II tactics and had absolutely no relevance to the Vietnamese war. We learned such things as the FEB, which signifies the Forward Edge of Battle and where to set up battalion aid stations. Of course, in Vietnam there was no FEB; casualties were evacuated directly from the field to a field hospital, a MASH or MUST unit (inflatable field hospitals). There were no battalion aid stations. Consequently, most of the first few days of training were a waste of time.

Toward the end of the first day, all of the doctors were lined up for inspection. Our leader said, "All of you who are specialists, take one step forward." A number of the surgeons, cardiologists, and others proudly stepped forward. Although I was a specialist in neurology, I did not move. Something in the back of my head was saying, "When in the Army, never volunteer." As it turned out, this was the right decision, because all of those who stepped forward were told they had to remain and clean up the area—picking up trash, cigarette butts, etc. I chose this opportunity to go and order my uniform and buy the necessary Army fatigues.

Next came the shot regime. We would stand in line to be given numerous shots; especially those of us who were going to Vietnam. We were inoculated against tetanus, typhoid, plague, and, of all things, smallpox, even though there had not been a case of smallpox in the world since 1957. Apparently, the military kept cultures of small pox alive because the Russians did. Both countries were afraid the other would use it during bacteriological warfare. My buddies and I had sore arms for the next few weeks. Vaccinations were not given by needle, but by a high-pressure air gun. It was relatively painless until the medicine was near the bottom of the bottle. In this case the gun would shoot foam instead of the high-pressure jet of vaccine and the foam was extremely painful. When people started hollering and complaining of severe pain, the Army knew it was time to change the bottle. It was a great example of quality control at its best.

In the second week of training we had lectures on tropical medicine, which I felt were of great value. This was the first time I started to pay attention. We learned about such things as scrub typhus, malaria, dengue fever, plague, rabies, cholera, and other exotic diseases. I would soon be diagnosing and treating these unusual diseases in large numbers.

The next phase of training was more to my liking. We learned how to use the weapons that would be assigned to us. These included the M-14 rifle and the 45-caliber side arm. Many of the doctors in my unit had never fired a weapon before, but I had been raised with various types of firearms. I was one of the better students. In the beginning, we learned how to aim and shoot without the use of bullets. The weapon was held in a vise, and we would sight down the barrel and a person would move the target. When we felt the target was on the bull's eye, we would say, "mark it." This way we could see how well we aimed our gun without firing a bullet.

The first time we had live ammunition and went on the firing range, we lined up and about ten people would sight their target and fire when given the order. After the first round was fired, it scared up a jackrabbit that ran in front of the targets. The instructor ordered no one to fire at the rabbit, but just about everyone did, which greatly angered him. I was the closest to him at the time and he asked me if I had fired at the rabbit. I quickly replied, "No sir." He wanted to know how he could believe I was telling the truth. I replied, "If I had been firing at the rabbit, he would be dead now," which made everyone laugh. Because of the rabbit's speed, I doubt that anyone on earth could have hit him and the instructor didn't appreciate my humor. The rest of that first day's practice went quite well and some of the other doctors actually hit their target. The instructor commented that we would not make good combat soldiers because so many of the targets went unscathed.

We next had field training in taking care of the wounded. This was mostly for the surgeons, but the Army wanted the rest of us to at least be familiar with the principles of wound debridement. A number of goats were anesthetized and shot. The surgeon would debride the wounds. We learned that taking care of wounds caused by high velocity projectiles was far different from anything surgeons had experienced in civilian life because of the amount of tissue damage done by the bullet from a high powered rifle.

While the surgeons were debriding the wounds, other physicians were taught how to perform a tracheotomy. We would take turns doing tracheotomies on the goat. A goat has a surprisingly long neck, so we could do four or five on the same animal. When we were all through debriding the wounds and doing the tracheotomy, the goat was euthanized and I believe it was donated to the local poor neighbors for dinner.

Our next training was about how to use a gas mask. We were instructed on how to put it on quickly. We were then taken into a large shed-like structure and the doors were closed. I thought it strange that the trees surrounding the shed were all painted white. Once inside the shed, we were instructed to hold our breath, put on the gas mask, breathe normally and walk around. The shed was filled with a strange, white haze. We quickly learned that this haze was real tear gas when we were ordered to take off our masks and give our name, rank, and serial number before exiting through lighted doors. The Army made sure we had an authentic experience.

It is hard to explain what it feels like to breathe tear gas. Your eyes burn and water so much that you can't keep them open. I now understood why the trees were painted white. As people staggered out of the shed, choking, coughing and with their eyes watering, they tended to run into these trees and the whiteness made them a little more visible.

We were also given a lecture on nerve gas and what to do if we were ever exposed to it. As nerve gas is invisible and odorless, the only way to tell if you are being gassed is if you see people in front of you falling over dead. If this happens you are instructed to put on your gas mask and inject yourself with a large syringe of atropine. The troops were required to carry atropine with them at all times and we received instructions on how to inject ourselves. We were instructed to take the large syringe, remove the top cover and thrust it into our anterior thigh directly through our clothing. The instructor asked for a volunteer to demonstrate this technique. It came as no surprise that no one volunteered. The instructor ordered an enlisted man, who was near by helping set up chairs, to show us how it was done. Having no choice, the enlisted man rapidly said, "Yes sir!" and immediately injected his thigh with the syringe, which made us glad we were not enlisted men.

FIELD TRAINING

With our basic classroom training over, it was time to get into our field gear and go off base for battlefield simulation training. We went through an infiltration course, which consisted of crawling combat style across the field under barbed wire just a few feet over us and navigating craters where explosive charges were planted. Machine guns fired live ammunition over our heads. We went from a ditch on one side of the field—probably about 40 yards—to a ditch on the other side of the field. An officer in a watchtower via remote control set off the charges. This was done so no one would be hurt; the officer could also control the machine gun in case someone panicked and stood up.

I was in the second wave that started across the field and because I was quite good at crawling on my belly (lots of practice from sneaking up on ducks in my youth), I was one of the first officers to cross to the other side. Being physicians, none of us took this exercise too seriously. Some of the ones who made it across the field started throwing dirt clods and rocks back at the ones still crawling. This play caused the officer in the watchtower to become quite upset. He had to stop the machine gun fire since he was afraid that a bullet would ricochet off one of the clods and cause bodily harm. Needless to say, a severe reprimand soon followed.

After the allotted time for traversing the course had passed, there were still a few doctors who had not made it across. In fact, there was an extremely portly OB-GYN doctor who had not gone more than 15 yards. The officer in charge stopped the exercise and let the remaining men walk over the course. We repeated this exercise once more after dark using tracer bullets. This was much more dramatic and a little scary because the bullets seemed so real compared to the "invisible" bullets of the daytime.

Next we had an exercise in map reading. We learned how to identify our location using a topographical map and compass. I saw great value to this exercise and paid careful attention to the instructor. I wanted to be able to tell people how to find me if I found myself in a position where I was lost or downed in a helicopter. We were told how to measure our steps so we would know how many yards or miles we had traveled. We were given a course where we had to change directions at least four times and end up finding a flag that had been placed on a fence. I was somewhat surprised at how accurately we could do this with just a compass and measuring our steps.

Once we completed our 4-day officer field training, we came back to the base and were given our assignments to our next base. While we all were headed for the same destination, some physicians were assigned to Vietnam immediately as replacement officers, while others were assigned to new units that were just forming. I was in the latter group.

OFFICER ON DECK

As my fellow officers and I soon learned, the Army was planning a huge military build-up of over 100,000 men and it was the practice to have medical units in place and functioning prior to the arrival of combat troops. This is why our class was so hurried. I was assigned to a new unit called the 98th medical detachment KO team that was to be formed at Valley Forge General Hospital in Pennsylvania. The Army wanted to create a new team combining neurology and psychiatry that was mobile and was able to deliver a real "punch" when needed, hence the term KO (knockout). My KO team was made up of three psychiatrists, two social workers, one psychologist, one neurologist, one mental health nurse, and fifteen enlisted personnel. We were given a few days' leave and then moved to Phoenixville, Pennsylvania where the hospital was located.

The unit (21 people), except for its officers, was already in place. I was the first officer to arrive so I became the temporary commanding officer (CO). The first day I arrived, the commanding base officer informed me that my unit met every morning at 0900 hours in a special designated area. When I showed up, everyone was already assembled.

The men in the unit came to attention and saluted me. In my role as CO, the ranking sergeant asked me what the unit would be doing that day. Having absolutely no idea what to tell them, I asked him what they did the day before. He reported, " They went swimming in the morning and played softball in the afternoon." I found no reason to change the pattern and quickly replied, "That is what we will do today then." I added some calisthenics to keep things interesting. We maintained this routine for four days. On the fifth day, the sergeant said "We are getting a little tired of this, let's do something else." I asked the sergeant for some ideas.

"We have a number of vehicles that came in for our unit; I think we should take them out and make sure they work OK," came his quick reply. I thought that was a reasonable request so I replied, " Let's go." Our equipment included a 2½-ton truck, an ambulance, some jeeps, and a smaller truck. This equipment supported our mobile unit; upon receiving orders, we could move everything at one time if needed.

We left base and planned to drive around in the countryside. We'd gotten about five miles outside of town when a state trooper stopped the lead vehicle and asked for the person in charge. The fingers pointed toward me, and the trooper asked for my convoy permit. When I said I didn't have one, the trooper promptly escorted us back to base where the CO, in no uncertain terms, told me I was not to leave base again. He also told me not to drive the vehicles because he didn't want them to break down before they were sent to Vietnam. Feeling it was important to know if they would operate well in Vietnam, I tried to reason with him—to no avail.

In the meantime, the rest of our equipment was arriving and I was required to sign for it in my role as the CO. I was not allowed to see the equipment, however, because it was classified. Every morning the sergeant would place new papers in front of me to sign. Since I had not received my security clearance, all information would be hidden—except for the signature line. I signed the forms hoping I would not be arrested at some later date. Later, when my security clearance finally arrived, I relaxed, knowing that I was signing for top secret things such as laundry detergent and toilet paper.

TOP SECRETS

I had fun playing the CO role for awhile. When the real CO showed up for our unit, I learned he out ranked me by only a matter of months; he had joined the Berry Plan. He knew a little more about command and organization than I did and I was happy to let him take over the command.

As there was little for me to do at this time, I looked up the neurologist at Valley Forge Hospital and helped him out by seeing patients. This was a valuable experience for me as many of these patients were casualties from Vietnam. The rest were typical neurological patients that one would see in any neurological practice. This was my first "real world" experience at treating neurological patients and it was exciting for me.

Meanwhile I brought my family down from Massachusetts and we stayed at a boarding house in Phoenixville. My wife and I knew I was going to Vietnam, but we had no idea when. Everything was top secret—as if there were North Vietnamese spies present. In fact, I was told not to tell anyone that I was a neurologist because the Army had one neurologist to care for every 100,000 troops. If the enemy found out another neurologist was being sent to Vietnam, they could figure out that the Army was going to increase its combat troops. It all seemed a little far-fetched to me but the Army seemed to take it seriously and therefore, so did I.

One thing I needed to do while in Phoenixville was to purchase items for my personal use that would not be available in Vietnam. I traveled to a large shopping mall in the nearby city called King of Prussia. I wanted to buy a tensor light to place near my bed. It only came with the bulb that was in it and I wanted some spare bulbs to take with me but I couldn't find any. I spoke with the saleslady about my predicament. She offered to order bulbs that would arrive within a week. I said, "I may not be here in a week as I'm on call to go overseas at any time." She asked what unit I was with and I replied, "the 98th medical detachment." She told me not to worry because this unit was not going to be shipped out until the middle of May. I asked her how she came by this top-secret information, as we in the unit were completely unaware of any timetable by which we would be sent to Vietnam. She said her daughter was a civilian secretary who worked in the command center at the hospital and she was the one who told her when my unit was leaving. As it turned out, she was absolutely correct as to when we were leaving so I got my spare bulbs. I thought to myself, "So much for top secret security!"

Before we left for Vietnam, the officers were supposed to become familiar with the use and care of a 45-caliber automatic sidearm. A lieutenant was assigned to teach us how to shoot a 45. As I was the only one who had ever shot a pistol before, I knew he had his work cut out for him. The lieutenant set a gallon can full of water about 20 paces away. We were supposed to shoot this can, and because it was full of water, it would show the great impact of a 45-caliber bullet. When no one in the unit could hit the can, the lieutenant moved us up to 10 paces. I finally managed to hit the can, but none of the other officers did. I do not think psychiatrists would have been much help during a firefight.

SHIPPING OUT

When the orders came that announced it was time for me to leave for Vietnam, I had eight hours to settle everything important. My unit was scheduled to leave in the morning and I moved quickly to get my things together, say good-bye to my family, and report to the base for a bus ride to the airport. As it turned out, our plane did not leave until nighttime, as it was the Army's policy to transport all personnel at night so that civilian personnel at the airport were not disrupted.

Our transportation was a commercial airliner that was chartered by the Army. Since our unit was small, we lucked out and they put us in first class. We flew to Chicago and arrived in the middle of the night. The airport looked like an armed camp with hundreds of soldiers milling about with their M14 rifles and other combat gear. We soon boarded a plane for Oakland, California; again riding first class. I took advantage of this opportunity to enjoy free drinks and fill the pockets of my bulky Army coat with a good number of "little bottles" of liquor.

My unit arrived in the morning along with many other planes. Our first step was to be processed out of country which entailed filling out numerous papers listing next of kin, whom to notify in case of injury or death, and the like. Everyone was bussed to a large troop ship that was birthed in the port of Oakland navy yard, named The General Green. The enlisted personnel were spot checked for bringing alcohol or other contraband onboard. The officers were allowed to go onboard without being checked, which was lucky for me, as my coat pockets were jangling from the numerous small liquor bottles.

Once on board we settled into our cabins. The officers had better quarters than the enlisted men. We had four double bunks to a room, while the enlisted men had bunks from the floor to the ceiling with about 16 inches of headspace in between and three to four men deep. Looking at the sleeping arrangement gave me a better understanding of what it might have felt like being on an eighteenth century slave ship.

As we were about to embark on our journey, a navy band came out to the end of the pier and played some rousing martial music for about 15 minutes. This was supposed to coincide with the ships pulling away from the docks. There were no other friends or family on the dock—just a few disinterested Navy personnel. When the band finished, they packed up and left. Meanwhile, the ship remained moored to the dock. About two hours later, the band reappeared, played the same music and then left again. A short time later, the ship pulled away from the dock. By now, the symbolism of this gesture was lost on most of the soldiers. I was later told that our departure delay was due to the height of the tide. The ship needed to pass under the Golden Gate Bridge at low tide and there had not been enough clearance earlier. I felt sad that there was not more of a coordinated send-off and official recognition for these hundreds of troops that were being sent to war.

LIFE ABOARD THE TROOP SHIP

*M*y troop ship headed across the San Francisco bay and passed under the Golden Gate Bridge beginning a long, boring transpacific journey. We experienced some of the roughest water during our first night. I was feeling more than a little seasick. By the second day out, it was much calmer and the ocean was smooth, although I cannot say I ever really felt great during the entire 30-day voyage.

The food was good for officers. I wish I could say as much for the enlisted men, but that would be a lie. I learned that enlisted men were told that their food was the same as officer food. This was true except that we had a choice of roast beef, turkey, or hot dogs, and the enlisted men were only offered hot dogs. Also, the officers sat down at tables with linen tablecloths and had waiters serve them. The enlisted men ate cafeteria style and they had to eat standing up by small, fold down trays that were connected to the ship walls. Usually as soon as the enlisted men finished one meal, they would get in line for the next because of the long time it took to feed them.

Life aboard the ship settled into a routine within about three days after leaving San Francisco. There was the predicted medical crisis of men going into delirium tremens or DTs since alcohol was not allowed on the ship. The men who were not withdrawing from alcohol or feeling seasick played games such as monopoly, bridge, and poker. In our unit, because so much anger and hostility was generated against the winners of monopoly, we tried to forbid officers from playing it. Movies were shown nearly every night without much variety. I saw Beach Blanket Bingo at least four times. I did not care for it the first time, but there was nothing else to do. I would have brought reading material, but we were only allowed so many pounds onboard. We had so much equipment that it took up most of the weight allowed.

Occasionally we would sight a whale. Everyone would rush to the side of the boat to view it. We had a kite-flying contest off the fantail. Otherwise there was little that happened. We had a little excitement a few days out from Guam when a typhoon entered our path. We had to divert about 100 miles or so off our course in order to avoid the serious part of it. There were some big waves and a lot of rain. I didn't get seasick, which surprised me. I guess that after a few weeks on the ship I had gotten my sea legs.

After we arrived in Guam for re-supply, the ship's crew had a memorial service for those who had lost their lives there during the Second World War. We then steamed on from Guam to South Vietnam. On this leg of the journey, I had my 31st birthday. The "little bottles" I brought with me enlivened my birthday party considerably as I had saved them all for this special occasion.

The rest of the trip was uneventful until we arrived at the coast of South Vietnam in a city called Vung Tau. There was an Army hospital at Vung Tau, which was said to be a coveted place to practice medicine as an Army doctor. We wondered if we would disembark here, since our destination was still a mystery. Some doctors came out of the hospital at Vung Tau, brought a bottle of Scotch and partied with us on our ship. I learned these physicians were hoping we would disembark at this spot since they were a little short-handed. We stayed anchored at this area for a few days while some combat troops were off-loaded. At night, we could see a destroyer, not far away, shelling an inland area. Guards were posted along the rails of our ship with rifles and orders to shoot at any type flotsam or jetsam just in case there was a Viet Cong frogman hiding in this trash in order to get close enough to the ship to place a mine on it. To my knowledge, there were no Viet Cong frogmen; however the shooting was a little nerve-wracking.

NEW HOME, NEW ROOMMATES, NEW JOB

*A*fter a couple of days of mooring at Vung Tau, the ship weighed anchor and we started traveling up the coast. The next stop was at Phan Thiet, where we unloaded more combat troops. We again moved up the coast to Phan Rang. Again, only combat troops were unloaded, as there were no medical facilities at this base.

Our next stop was Cam Ranh Bay. We were all hoping this would be our final destination as it was a large base, an up-to-date hospital, and it was said to be extremely secure. We were disappointed to learn that we would not disembark until we reached Nha Trang about 20 miles north.

We gathered all our gear and we were off-loaded onto an amphibious landing craft—just like John Wayne in his movie, *The Sands of Iwo Jima*. We were burdened with all of our equipment; each of us had a 70-pound duffel bag, M14 rifle, 45-caliber pistol, shelter half (half a pup tent), gas mask, and five days' supply of C rations. We felt like we were going into combat. In the distance inland, we could see black smoke drifting toward the clear-blue skies. After seeing the smoke we felt sure we were going into combat, and the war was beginning to feel very real.

The landing craft finally made it to the beach. The front end went down and we disembarked into soft sand. The temperature was at least 105 degrees. After struggling for 20 yards, we were exhausted. I was surprised to see Army personnel on the beach in bathing suits sipping cold beer and staring at us like we had just arrived from Mars. One man, an officer, came toward us and said, "Where in the hell do you think you're going with all that stuff?" He told us to leave our equipment on the ground and he would "have it picked up." To my surprise, he then invited us to join him for some cold beer. We later learned that the black smoke that caused us fear was actually caused from burning off the latrines, which was done every day or so. When I asked the officer about the smoke, he replied, "We call that stuff SMIT." I asked what that meant. He replied, "In Los Angeles, a combination of smoke and fog is called Smog. You figure it out." I enjoyed my beer, and I left my equipment on the beach as instructed. That was the last time I saw my shelter half, gas mask, the C rations and other equipment. To this day, I have no idea what happened to them.

After a cold beer in the officers club, we were taken to our new home, which was called a villa. This villa was a reasonably nice stucco home that had five bedrooms, a large common room and a bathroom with a shower. These structures were apparently built by the Vietnamese and leased to the Americans to house officers. The officers from our KO team all lived in the same villa. Two officers were assigned to one room. Two officers were already in the villa and I learned they were assigned to the Nike anti-aircraft missile base which was near to us.

I roomed with a Psychiatrist who suffered from night terrors. I quickly learned that he would dash around the room in the middle of the night thinking that there were Viet Cong coming in through the windows. While all officers were assigned rifles, we decided early on that my roommate would be disarmed because of this medical condition. I was allowed to keep my 45-caliber pistol in order to protect the villa. I kept it under my pillow at night so that my roommate could not find it during one of his night terrors. The roommate had no recollection of the night terrors in the morning. I would usually take care of him when he had them, and, except for my CO, our other roommates did not know about them.

The villa was on the edge of town, not far from the 8th Field Hospital. Our unit had yet to establish a building to work in so we were given lumber and large tents. We were expected to build our own facilities for seeing patients in a place called Camp McDermont, named after a private who was killed there a few years earlier during a surprise attack. I was not at all happy with this arrangement for a couple of reasons. I did not like the idea of examining patients in a tent environment. I wanted a more stable hospital environment with equipment and supplies. Even through they were not part of my unit, I knew that I would work closely with the Neurosurgeons and Internists, and I wanted to be near them.

For these reasons, I quickly disassociated myself from my unit and sought to establish an office at the 8th Field Hospital. A psychiatrist, who had finished his tour of duty and was going home, vacated a nice office. It was one of the few offices in the entire hospital that was air-conditioned, and I quickly claimed it. I felt lucky in establishing myself there. It was right by the main receiving area of the 8th Field Hospital. Having established roots, I started seeing patients within a few days. I never went back to Camp McDermont, which was usually referred to as "Tent City."

My unit inquired about the location of our large equipment. We learned that someone else had appropriated our vehicles except for one jeep. The CO told us we didn't need the other trucks as the Army had other uses for them. He told us that we would not be moving unlike some other units who were mobile, similar to the one in the Alan Alda movie, *M*A*S*H*. We were grateful to at least have our jeep so we could drive to the officers' club for dinner each night. My new life in Vietnam was beginning to take form as I began my year of duty.

A LITTLE WHITE LIE

*E*arly in the War, it was decided that when troops were deployed to Vietnam, their families would be allowed to move; in fact, they were encouraged to move, anywhere in the continental United States, and the Army would pay for it. This decision was made because of something that happened at Fort Campbell, Kentucky. This was the home base for a large number of soldiers who died in Vietnam. After bodies were flown home and one funeral after another was held, the emotional impact proved devastating for the families and for the friends who became family because of their close living relationships and ties to the war.

When I was sent to Vietnam, my wife decided she wanted to move as far away from Massachusetts as possible and she chose California. In order for her to accomplish this move, she needed a copy of the orders that sent me to Vietnam. As mentioned previously, I had no orders except for a lengthy telegram. She sent a letter asking me to help her resolve this dilemma.

I spoke to our unit's clerk typist and had him make me a copy of this telegram and I sent it to my wife post haste. I received a letter by return mail saying they would not accept this telegram—the Army needed a copy of my orders to prove that I was in Vietnam. I met with my company commander, Colonel Hall, and asked him to make up a set of orders sending me to Vietnam. He said he would not issue orders because it was stupid: I was already in Vietnam. He could not order me to some place where I was already. Without proof that I was in Vietnam, the Army would not pay for my wife to move. With this dilemma in mind, I decided I would deal with this in the Army way: I would try to bribe someone.

I asked the clerk typist to type up some "orders," and in return, I offered to give him four frozen steaks and the use of a jeep for half a day. He agreed to type my "orders" but told me he couldn't sign them, only Colonel Hall could sign the "orders." While the young clerk typist would not forge Colonel Hall's name, he was full of ideas. He told me that the colonel had a huge stack of things to sign every morning. The next day he would delay bringing the colonel's coffee until after the colonel signed all the morning documents. The clerk typist believed this coffee delay would sufficiently nudge Colonel Hall to quickly sign the papers—including my orders, since he required his early morning Java fix. The ploy worked beautifully and I got my orders signed. Although this was illegal, I felt I was on moral high ground because, after all, I was in Vietnam at the time and my wife needed help. My wife got her moving funds eventually, and she enjoyed her adventure traveling across the country with my young daughter, Christina.

WHAT YOUR BRAIN HEARS

*T*he first night after arriving in Vietnam when I tried to sleep, I kept hearing large explosions every 30 to 40 minutes. I asked the men who had been living in the villa for six months to explain the tremendous noise. I learned it was "H & I" fire. I quickly learned that "H & I" stood for "Harassment and Interdict" artillery fire. The noise resulted from the artillery fire going overhead every 30 to 40 minutes into "no man's land" throughout the night. The artillerymen would zero in on spots that were crossroads or other natural thoroughfare, such as riverbeds or suspected enemy encampments that were identified earlier in the day by spotter planes. This indiscriminate firing did little damage to the enemy except to keep them awake at night. Unfortunately, the noise was loud and it kept me awake too. I also had a fear that the rounds might fall short and land on us by accident.

My experienced colleagues told me I would get used to this noise and, as unbelievable as it may seem, I did. I found that after a couple of weeks, I could sleep through the night without ever waking up—with one exception. One night after I had been in Vietnam a few months, I sat suddenly upright in my bed not knowing what woke me. I heard a muffled explosion followed by six more explosions that were caused by incoming mortar fire that was targeting our helicopter base. I was told the next day that there were a total of eight rounds fired and apparently the first one woke me up. Although the sound was probably a tenth as loud as the artillery shells going out, the fact that it was incoming and represented danger aroused me instantly. I learned that the Viet Cong (VC) only fire a short number of mortar rounds and then leave rapidly because of the ability and technology at the U.S. base, which could electronically trace the incoming rounds and triangulate their source. We could then direct our artillery fire and blanket the source of the incoming mortar fire. A pattern soon developed: the VC would fire a few rounds and they would retreat quickly. The only time the VC outwitted us with this technique was when they set up a mortar on top of a building in downtown Nha Trang because they knew we would not retaliate with artillery fire at the center of the city.

The interest of this story is about the human ability to adapt to noise. It proves how you can become attuned to certain noises and block them out during sleep, but other noises—even though they are much quieter—will wake you up. This correlates to how a mother will wake up when she hears her own child crying but may sleep through radio, TV, and other louder noises. This ability to wake up proves that, from a neurological point of view, your brain is alert during sleep as well as when you're awake.

SERENDIPITY

*B*efore leaving the United States for Vietnam, my unit had collectively purchased some large items that were to be shipped ahead of us to our final destination. These items included things we wanted but did not think we could buy in Vietnam. One item was a small, three-foot refrigerator. Unfortunately the refrigerator did not arrive by the time we arrived so several people in my unit proceeded to trace its whereabouts.

It did not take us long to learn that the refrigerator was appropriated by an officer who was in charge of shipping these types of things. We were unsure why he had taken this action. We guessed that it was either for profit, since a refrigerator could bring a good price in Vietnam, or the officer simply wanted a refrigerator for his own use. Either way we were angry. We raised such a stink that the person in charge of shipment and supply told us not to worry; he would replace our refrigerator.

A few days later a large truck delivered a huge refrigerator that stood about seven feet tall. Since the one we lost was only about three feet tall we were quite pleased until we learned the appliance was a large stand-up freezer—not a refrigerator.

My colleagues and I pondered this unfortunate turn of events and considered what to make of it since the primary item we wanted to store in our new refrigerator was beer. We came up with two ideas that improved our outlook about this situation. First, we knew that the electricity in Vietnam was unreliable because of our lights frequently going off and on. It was our guess that the freezer would never quite freeze given this electricity dilemma. Second, we could turn the freezer up to its warmest settings. We felt that the combination of these ideas might just keep our items from freezing.

The seven-foot freezer turned out to be a better appliance than the three-foot refrigerator, which would probably not have kept things cold because of the unreliable electricity. We enjoyed our ice-cold beer with occasional ice crystals that would form when we opened the container. This experience taught us to be creative, and to trust our instincts while in Vietnam.

TEMPORARY DUTY

*A*bout two weeks after I arrived at the 8th Field Hospital, the CO of my medical unit ordered me to go on TDY (temporary duty) down to a place called Long Bin, just north of Saigon, to replace the neurologist who was working there. This neurologist was the only one in Vietnam and he was going to Japan for two weeks of rest and relaxation and to provide some medical assistance. I was upset, and maybe a little bit frightened, to be separated from my unit and the people I knew, to travel in a hostile country to an unknown place and be with people I did not know. But orders were orders, so I had to go.

My mode of transportation was a C-123 cargo plane. I had never flown in a cargo plane and I found it to be an unpleasant experience. The plane was loaded with cargo that consisted of a jeep and other equipment. Flying in military aircraft is particularly unnerving for several reasons. When you first get on the airplane, you complete a card with the name, address, and phone number of someone to notify in case of death. When the time came for passengers to board the plane, we had to walk up the back ramp, which was an awkward feeling. When I got inside and looked for my seat, I discovered there were none. The experienced travelers ran for the vehicles in the plane and jumped in the seats. I was left with combat seating which consisted of pipes running along the lower body of the plane about 12 inches out and about 18 inches high. Between the side of the plane and this pipe ran a line of netting with straps about two feet apart. I was expected to sit inside this netting and dangle as though I were in a hammock. I strapped myself in and said prayers I remembered from childhood.

The engines started up after everything was secured and the noise was unbelievable. This was a twin engine turbo-prop plane with no insulation. The person next to me was a sergeant who had flown many times and he was a rather jovial sort of fellow. He told me not to worry because the plane was safe. Safe was an unusual word to use considering there were snipers at the end of the runway who would shoot at us as we took off. I asked him why the Army did not get rid of the shooters, and he replied, "Because the one who is there now was a poor shot, and the Army is afraid if they got rid of him, the Vietnamese will get someone else who is more skilled." I later learned that this was a standard joke that was told to all cargo plane virgins, especially if they were captains. Unfortunately, I believed him and I was petrified. I felt grateful that we took off without a shot being fired. We proceeded on our way south with stops at Phan Rang, Phan Thiet, and on to our final destination of Bin Hoa, which was a large American-controlled airfield.

Upon arrival at Bin Hoa, I had no idea where to go or what to do. I showed my orders to the nearest person who looked like an officer, and he directed me to the ground transport section. When I arrived there, I showed my orders to the communication corporal who said he would call a jeep to have me transported to Long Bin if it was not too late. I anxiously said, "What do you mean if it isn't too late?" He replied, "The road is not secure after dark and it is swept for land mines every eight hours, and I don't know when the last sweep occurred." This information did not calm the high level of anxiety that I was already experiencing. A jeep did arrive soon and my driver told me we would be completely safe to drive to Long Bin at this time of day. So off we went toward my new temporary home and assignment, although I noted that the driver carried an M-14 rifle next to him in the jeep.

MY NEW HOSPITAL

A 45-minute drive through rice paddies and jungle got me to the new hospital in Long Bin where I was ordered to report for temporary duty. My driver and I arrived at the 93rd evacuation hospital, which had literally been carved out of the jungle. Compared to where I had come from in Nha Trang, this hospital was less than what I expected. The 93rd hospital facility had few of the amenities I had experienced at the 8th Field Hospital. The medical officers were housed in a huge Quonset hut and each officer was assigned his own space, which was about 15 by 10 feet with no walls. A line on the floor signified my space for privacy. I moved into the space that was vacated by Dr. Daroff, the neurologist whom I was replacing.

The bathroom facilities were much like the latrines that the enlisted men had at Camp McDermott. When we got up in the morning, we would stand at a long wooden bar and wash our faces and shave with water placed in a helmet. I felt that this was primitive and outdated: I had seen that technique in WWII movies. The office where I was to work was in a freshly constructed wooden building that was about 10 by 10 feet with a low ceiling—and very hot. There was no air conditioning anywhere in the 93rd evacuation hospital.

Most of the patients I saw were from the first infantry division, "the big red one." After the first day of seeing patients, I felt I had been sent to hell. I immediately sought out an officers club and much to my disappointment, there was none to be found. The NCO's (non-commissioned officers) had built a small hooch where they served drinks and some food and they invited me to join them for happy hour. After a couple of drinks, things didn't look quite so bad. I was told not to loiter outside the club while it was still light because in the past few weeks they had taken some sniper fire. Immediately I did not feel so good anymore and I returned to my Quonset hut. Feeling unbearably hot and sweaty, I asked my neighbors where I could take a shower. They said, "Right now you can't, because the nurses are showering." It turned out that the showers were exactly like we saw on the *M*A*S*H* TV series. They consisted of wooden structures with canvas sides and an overhead shower with a pull cord. There was no hot water and it was not missed.

While I was waiting my turn to shower, everyone vacated the Quonset hut. When I asked where folks were going someone replied, "We're going to see tonight's movie." I learned that the movie was held outdoors with chairs set up for the viewers and a sheltered hut for the projectionist. My colleagues had barely left the hut before it started to rain heavily.

I soon learned that I was beginning to experience the rainy season in South Vietnam. Almost every day at this time the sky would open up and rain would fall extremely hard. I went out and saw everyone sitting in the rain waiting for the movie and I thought they were all crazy. Within two days, I was sitting out there with them, as the rain was warm and actually felt good. When the rain ended, steam would rise from the ground due to the intense heat. The Vietnamese jungle had the feel of a Hollywood special effects stage. After the movie, I went back to my small space in the Quonset hut to try to get some sleep.

While at this new hospital I learned just how far full grown, well-educated physicians could regress when they are depressed. If I set one foot or let my chair stray across the floor line into someone else's territory, my colleagues would become enraged. I quickly learned to stay within my designated boundary. Outside of the Quonset hut with its designated boundaries, the other doctors were quite cordial, friendly, and even helpful.

While detached to the 935th medical detachment KO team, I grew to like and respect my colleagues. I saw some interesting patients and made neurology presentations to the medical group, which were appreciated. While I was there, quite a few casualities arrived, and although I was not directly involved with taking care of these patients, I did get some experience as a triage officer. I was impressed with one of the celebrities who visited our hospital: John Wayne. Most of the celebrities who came to visit the casualities would go through the hospital after the patients were operated on, cleaned up, and well bandaged. But John Wayne was right out there visiting with them as they arrived by helicopter. I recalled one young man—probably 18 or 19 years old—who was badly wounded by multiple fragment wounds resulting from a mortar attack. John Wayne went up to his litter (a stretcher) as he was being carried into the triage area and said, "Geeze kid, you look like hell," whereupon the soldier responded with a big grin on his face, "Wow, Duke, can I have your autograph?" Wayne readily gave the soldier his autograph, and said "These doctors are the best in the world and you'll be OK!" I believe that comment did more for this young soldier's morale then anything the doctors could have done.

After a brief ten-day stay in Long Bin I was given orders to return to the 98th medical detachment in Nha Trang. Dr. Daroff was returning from his vacation, and he would resume his assignment. I was happy to return to my 8th Field Hospital, my villa, and my unit.

THE JOY OF BEING A COMMANDING OFFICER

*A*fter a 10-day stay in Long Bin, I was ready to return to the 8th Field Hospital. I left on a flight out from Bin Hoa, and the airplane traced its previous route back to Nha Trang-with one big exception. I was informed that after Phan Thiet and Phan Rang, we were traveling to Da Nang, which bypassed my destination of Nha Trang. I learned that Da Nang was the destination of several senior officers on board. After taking these senior officers to Da Nang, the plane would retrace the flight pattern, halfway down the country to Nha Trang. Besides adding two hours to an already uncomfortable flight, this flight change worried me as I had heard there were frequent attacks on airplanes coming in and out of Da Nang.

As it turned out, when we stopped at Phan Rang we picked up casualties that had been involved in a recent ambush by the Viet Cong. I quickly learned that as soon as an airplane or any other vehicle takes on casualties; the ranking medical officer takes charge of the aircraft or vehicle. Since I was the only medical officer on board, this meant I was in charge despite the fact that there were two Majors, a Lieutenant Colonel, and a Bird Colonel on board. Once the medical passengers were loaded on board, the airplane captain came back and asked me for orders. I seized the opportunity and told him that one of the injured men had a sucking chest wound that required immediate attention. This assessment was partially true. A medic had placed a Vaseline gauze dressing over the wound, which had prevented it from being a sucking wound—but no one else knew this fact. I said, "This man must be taken care of in a field hospital as soon as possible." After hearing this information, the patient became justifiably alarmed. I bent down and whispered in his ear that he would be OK. I asked the patient, "You want to be in a clean bed with good food and nurses taking care of you as soon as possible, don't you?" "Yeah, I sure do," he quietly replied. I asked him to just play along with me, where upon he clutched his chest and began to moan loudly. I told him not to overdo it and he quieted down. The closest field hospital was Nha Trang, which brought me home without having to travel through Da Nang. While the other superior officers complained, fretted, and fumed because they wanted to go directly to their destination in Da Nang, it did them no good because I was the ranking medical officer.

When we arrived at Nha Trang, there was an ambulance waiting for us because the captain had radioed ahead to describe our medical emergency. I told the ambulance driver that I needed to ride with the patient to the 8th Field Hospital because the patient had a sucking chest wound. After looking at the patient and looking quizzically at me, the driver followed my orders. When we arrived at the 8th Field Hospital, a thoracic surgeon met the patient and gave him a brief examination. After the exam, he looked up at me said, "This patient does not have a sucking chest wound!" I replied, "What do I know, I'm only a neurologist." And that was all that was said about the incident. Within 15 minutes, I arrived at my villa safely and was enjoying a cold beer.

NUNG GUARDS

*U*pon arriving back to my villa in Nha Trang after a 10-day assignment in Long Bin, I found that things had changed. There was a large tent in our front yard that housed two Nung guards. Nung guards are indigenous Chinese people who live in Vietnam but had refused to fight in the Vietnamese Army because they were always given the most odious and dangerous assignments. Rather than cause internal strife, the Americans hired them as mercenaries for guard duty and other less hazardous assignments. The Nung guards were guarding my villa because of an interesting event that occurred while I was in Long Bin.

Apparently, my roommate had one of his night terrors. He screamed that the Viet Cong were attacking him. This woke up all residents in the villa and everyone ran around trying to find the perpetrators. In the process, they woke up my roommate who had no idea what was going on and he subsequently joined in the search. Of course, they found no one and the next day the unit requested round-the-clock guards. The request was granted, and two Nung guards, Pan and Lu, were assigned to us. Pan and Lu lived in the tent outside our villa and "guarded us" twenty-four hours a day. They cooked and ate their meals on a small hibachi, and they were provided with a ration of rice, as they had little else to eat. Whenever I could, I brought them food in "doggie bags" from the officers club or a restaurant. Although I was told not to do this, I felt it was the only decent thing to do, as they had little or no protein in their diet.

Pan and Lu lacked ability and know-how in terms of what it meant to be a guard. They were issued a 12-gauge pump shotgun and five shells. One day I took them aside and asked them to show me how to use a shotgun. They handed it to me and shook their heads indicating that they had no idea how to load or use a shotgun. Having been a duck hunter, I knew exactly how to use this type of shotgun. I took the weapon, looked into the chamber and found there was no shell inside. I pumped it twice and found there were no shells in the tube. This incident both alarmed and dismayed me. It proved to me that Pan and Lu had no idea what they were doing. I showed them how to load and aim the weapon and asked them why they were not taught how to complete this task. Although their English was limited, I got the impression that their CO did not trust them with a loaded weapon; I tended to agree. I also felt that if we ever were attacked, Pan and Lu would disappear within minutes or probably seconds. Although the other officers in my group felt secure having twenty-four hour guard protection, I knew better. Pan and Lu did have one positive contribution. They kept the local kids from vandalizing our villa while we were gone during the day.

NEW PATIENTS; NEW CHALLENGES

At the 8th Field Hospital in Nha Trang, I usually saw patients between 9:00 A.M. through 12:00 P.M. The rest of the time I was mostly on my own. The type of patients I saw were quite similar to the type I would see in any neurology practice, with one exception. These patients, by virtue of their age and physical fitness, were much healthier than a normal panel of neurological patients having obviously been screened for neurological disease or any other major problem before being sent to Vietnam.

Having my afternoons and evenings free led me to become somewhat bored, so I volunteered to see patients at the local province hospital near downtown Nha Trang. The Vietnamese ran this hospital with considerable help from U.S. supplies and American doctors who volunteered to work with them for up to one year. As the Vietnamese had no neurologist, I was welcomed to evaluate patients in their hospitals including the ARVIN hospitals, which were the local military Vietnamese hospitals. Most American doctors from the Army hospital were not welcome in the Vietnamese hospitals because the Vietnamese doctors represented the specialties, such as Internal Medicine. The local doctors did not want the competition, or especially the loss of face, if the Army doctors turned out to be more skilled in diagnoses and treatment. Being a neurologist, there was no competition and therefore no loss of face if I made a diagnosis and suggested a treatment that they had not considered.

I began a clinical practice in both the province hospital and in the ARVIN hospital once a week. My Vietnamese colleagues would identify patients who they felt would be of neurological interest and have them come back on my clinic day. If the patient happened to arrive on the day after I left, he or she would often camp out on the hospital grounds and wait for me until the following week.

The Vietnamese patients held physicians in high esteem and I was told that physicians were called "Bac Si" which translates into "most learned one." I saw interesting cases consisting of plague meningitis, cholera, rabies, leprosy, and rare tropical diseases that I had never seen previously. One of the first patients I examined appeared to be in a deep coma and had been in that state for two days. I had no idea what her problem was, but as part of my examination I opened up one of her eyes and looked in with my ophthalmoscope. I looked into her right eye, then her left. After I viewed the left eye, she suddenly awoke—to everyone's amazement—including mine. From that point on, my reputation was made and all the patients with any kind of illness wanted me to look into their eye with my "magic machine." In retrospect, I think her coma was caused by an overdose of narcotics that her mother had bought over the counter. The patient probably had been given an injudicious amount for a stomachache. I was just at the right place at the right time when the narcotic wore off.

In that same first week, I saw a 15-year-old girl who was suffering from dystonia affecting her right arm. This condition made it difficult for her to do her job, which was placing small stones in potholes to repair roads. These stones had to be placed with care and skill so they would fill the pothole with a smooth and interlocking surface. With dystonia, she found it difficult to do this. I placed her on Valium, which seemed to work well to relieve her symptoms to the extent that she could do her job. She was so grateful for this treatment that she was always at my clinic and insisted on carrying my bag in gratitude.

My visit to the ARVIN hospital was somewhat different. Because this was a military hospital, the physicians were more sensitive about "losing face." When I arrived at the hospital, I was invited into a small dining room where I was served tea, fresh fruit, and some other snacks. The physicians and I talked about local matters in the town, or how the war was going. We generally just chitchatted for about an hour. Then, as I was about to leave, the doctor would say, "By the way, we have a patient with a neurological problem that you may want to see." The doctor would bring in a patient whom I remembered sitting in the waiting room when I first arrived. After examining the patient and making a diagnosis, I would recommend a treatment. I would tell them that I had learned about this from Dr. An, who ran the local province hospital. This humble approach fostered communication and built relationships, and it got me invited back the following week—something no one else had accomplished.

On another occasion, things did not work out so well. The Vietnamese physicians showed me a patient who was having seizures. After my examination, I found the patient to have classic symptoms of sub-acute bacterial endocarditis. He had a loud heart murmur and flame-shaped hemorrhages in the nail beds. He was being treated with inadequate doses of antibiotics and I told the physicians this patient required immediate treatment of massive doses of antibiotics. This seemed to cause them to "lose face," and I was not invited back for three weeks. When I returned and asked about the patient, the physicians told me they did not know what happened to him. I was never allowed to see any other patients who had infections.

The local province hospital was located on Yersin Street. This not being a Vietnamese name, I asked where it came from. The chief of staff at the province hospital said he thought it was named after a Frenchman as there was a Pasteur clinic in the city of Nha Trang which had been there for many years and had been managed by the French. I later looked up the name Yersin and found that he had been a student of Louis Pasteur and had first isolated the plague bacillus in Nha Trang, Vietnam. So Nha Trang does have a claim to fame in the medical history books.

In 1966, Bubonic plague was prevalent in Vietnam and I saw many cases during my tour of duty. Except for the pneumonic or menegitic form, the plague was easy to treat. A short course of tetracycline was usually all that was needed to cure the disease.

We discovered an interesting problem when treating patients in the outpatient department of the province hospital: patients liked to trade pills once they left the clinic. I learned that yellow, pink, or white pills were more highly regarded than blue, orange, or brown. The Vietnamese refused to take a pill if it was black. We found an easy solution. Whenever possible, we would give injections rather than prescribe pills.

Another patient of interest was a young boy who had a rare genetic disorder of osteogenesis imperfecta that causes the bones to break spontaneously. The disease has an unusual finding of blue sclera. However, this boy's sclera was green because he also had jaundice from hepatitis. Ever since seeing this patient, I have taken delight in stumping my medical students by asking what condition gives you green sclera. No one has ever guessed correctly.

One last example of a challenge involved the cholera ward. The ward was a freestanding building with one big room and a cement floor that sloped toward the street where there was a drain. The room had cots with holes in the center. The patient's butt would fit into the hole. The patients had IV fluids that contained antibiotics running into both arms and sometimes into both feet. Urine and diarrhea would fall onto the floor and flow to one side of the room where lye was spread over it as a disinfectant. The sewage would drain out of the facility and into the street. The patients seemed to do well since cholera is a self-limiting disease if you can keep the patient from dying from dehydration. The technique was crude, but efficient.

THE JEEP

*R*elationships between my villa-mates and I were becoming somewhat strained because they worked in "Tent City" and I worked in an air-conditioned office in the 8th Field Hospital. In the evening we could never agree on where to eat. There was always a big hassle and we had to vote every night since we only had one vehicle. I enjoyed traveling downtown to dine at the local restaurants. My roommates never wanted to go downtown but wanted to stay local and eat at the officers club. Every night I was outvoted. As soon as a spot opened up in the housing that was located on the 8th Field Hospital compound, I was determined to move so I would not need transportation to go to and from work. Luckily, there was soon an opening, and the physician who vacated the spot had a jeep that he left in my care. This was a godsend, as it provided me with transportation, as well as a bargaining tool.

Since no one knew where this jeep came from and it did not belong to any particular unit, the doctors at the 8th Field Hospital decided to share it. Our only problem was obtaining gasoline. When you took a vehicle into the motor pool to have it fueled, paperwork was required that named my unit and the registration number on the jeep—information that we did not have. I solved this problem by bribing the mess sergeant to give me four frozen steaks. In exchange, he got to use the jeep for a day. I used the four steaks to bribe the motor pool private who refueled the vehicles. This may not have been the most honest way to get things done, but it was the Army way.

The jeep came in handy for many reasons. It was not really mine, but I seemed to be in charge of it. I traveled to places that I would not have seen if not for the jeep. One of the places I visited was a restaurant called

Forgets, which had excellent French food, although the wine that came from Algeria, was not very good. Another favorite dining spot was called Beach House #1. It was a small open-air restaurant on the beach and they specialized in seafood. The first time I ate there, I ordered prawns and I was brought a huge crustacean on a plate. I told them, "Not lobster, I want prawn." A Chinese gentleman, who spoke little English, ran the restaurant. He kept pointing at my dinner and said, "prawn, prawn." When I looked more closely at my dinner, I beheld the largest shrimp I had ever seen in my life. It was also the most delicious shrimp I had ever eaten. I asked the Chinese gentleman if all the shrimp were that big. His daughter, who spoke more English and acted as a translator, told me not always. Sometimes her father had to put two shrimp on a plate for dinner. As one can imagine, this restaurant became a favorite dining place for me while stationed in Vietnam.

There was another good seafood restaurant about four miles south of Nha Trang but I was told I would have to be out of the village by nightfall as the road was unsafe. Eventually the road was closed altogether since it had been mined on one occasion, and the Army did not feel it was a military necessity to keep the road open. There were other small restaurants downtown that I visited, which had authentic Vietnamese food. I found most food bland and not to my liking with one exception: Nuoc-mam. This delicacy is fermented fish sauce. I am told it smells rancid, but it tasted delicious to me and it spiced up my food. Good Chinese food was also available. No restaurant served silverware so I quickly became an expert with using chopsticks. I'm grateful my little jeep took me to these unique places during my tour of Vietnam.

THE ROAD TO CAM RANH BAY

*W*hen I first arrived in Vietnam, Americans could drive between Nha Trang and Cam Ranh Bay, which is about 15 miles, and feel relatively safe even though the Viet Cong theoretically controlled the area. However, on the trip to Cam Ranh Bay we were routinely stopped twice—first, a few miles outside of Nha Trang and second, a few miles from Cam Ranh Bay. These were roadblocks that were set up and manned by men in the typical garb of VC, which to us looked like black pajamas. These guards were armed and they required us to pay a toll that usually amounted to a couple of dollars in their currency. Other than that, the road was safe; there were no snipers and it was not mined. I don't know if these people were actually Viet Cong soldiers or just local farmers who were being entrepreneurs. The Army decided it was unwise and ridiculous to pay toll to the enemy to allow our vehicles to use the road, so we gave the VC notice that the U.S. would no longer pay a toll for the use of the road. The U.S. traveled down the road with armed vehicles and tore down the blockades and chased away the toll-takers. From that time on, we paid no toll but the road was unsafe to travel because it was mined and there was sniper fire. It probably would have been much cheaper to pay the toll then it was to have to sweep the road for mines every day and be forced to travel in larger armed convoys.

The medical personnel, who used to travel down to Cam Ranh Bay to provide psychiatric and neurological support for the hospital, could no longer do so unless we traveled by helicopter. For me, flying by helicopter was scarier then traveling on the road because the helicopter had to fly at either high altitudes or at tree-top level to avoid sniper fire, and the helicopters usually traveled over water. Helicopters were flown with doors open, and frequently the only thing between the water and me was a seat belt. The helicopter pilots seemed to take great delight in scaring the medical officers as we flew to Cam Ranh Bay.

THE KOREANS

*N*ot long after my tour of duty in Vietnam began, the Koreans sent over a division of fighting men to aid the Americans. It was little known or recognized in the United States that the Koreans had a full division of troops in Vietnam called the White Horse division. The Koreans proceeded with the build-up of troops just as the Americans had done—by sending over their medical unit first. The fighting men soon followed.

The Koreans began fighting in the war before their designated hospital was completed. Since the Koreans were building their hospital a few miles north of Nha Trang, those who were injured before the completion of their own hospital were brought to the American hospital for treatment. Some of the Korean doctors were assigned to the 8th Field Hospital; they acted as interpreters and treated some of the Korean casualties. I became a close friend of two of these doctors. On one occasion, prior to the assignment of the Korean doctors to the 8th Field Hospital, some Korean casualties were brought in for treatment. Although I was not on duty at the time, I was called in to meet the helicopter delivering the casualties. The Korean field unit had radioed ahead to relay information about a soldier with an eye injury. Because we had no ophthalmologist at the 8th Field Hospital, the commanding officer decided that the neurologist was the closest thing that the United States had to an ophthalmologist. So I was assigned to greet the helicopter and evaluate the patient, despite my protest that I had little ophthalmology knowledge.

The patient did have an eye injury; in fact, he had no eye whatsoever. He had a terrible head injury and was in a deep coma. I immediately called for an anesthesiologist to intubate the patient to relieve his labored breathing. I held his head while the anesthesiologist inserted the breathing tube. Once he was stabilized I sent him immediately to the x-ray unit. The results of the x-rays disclosed a large metallic object that appeared to be inside the Korean's head. I felt this was probably a blood pressure mechanism that had carelessly been left under his head when the x-ray was taken. However, the x-ray technologist pointed out to me that if I were to carefully examine the AP and the lateral views of the x-ray, I would see that this object was indeed inside his head. I had no idea what this object was but I had a strong, uneasy feeling that it was something bad.

I called for some ordinance people who looked at the x-rays and told me "What we have here is an unexploded M79 rifle grenade." The triggering mechanism was lodged under the super-orbital ridge. I did not understand the technical details of how rifle grenades were armed and exploded, but I was left with the distinct impression that we were all in grave danger while handling this patient. The ordinance people strongly suggested that we place sandbags around the patient since the grenade could explode at any time. This rifle grenade had entered through the left eye and was not visible from the outside. It had caused a serious fracture in the soldier's skull causing it to open and close as the grenade entered the head—much like a clamshell.

I called the neurosurgeons to ask if they wanted to operate and remove this grenade. After looking at the x-rays, they decided to have nothing more to do with the soldier. I was told to place him on the expectant list which, in military terms, means the patient was expected to die and nothing else could be done for him. The other doctors and I followed this recommendation. The soldier was placed behind a wall of sandbags and in three to four hours he died.

Once the soldier died, another problem surfaced—how to dispose of his remains. Since he was a Korean national, we called the Korean commander and advised him that he could remove the remains. After noting the situation, the Koreans replied that they had no ordinance people and they gave us permission to take care of the remains. As we had no mechanism for taking care of foreign nationals, the U.S. commanders decided to hold a high-level conference with the Korean commanders to find a solution. It was decided that because we had ordinance experts, we would cut off the soldier's head and return the rest of the body back to the Koreans. The ordinance people called our pathologist and told him to cut off the soldier's head. After evaluating the situation, the pathologist replied "This is not part of my job" and he refused to do it. Another high-level conference was held. It was then decided that the soldier's body would be frozen to prevent random head movement. Once frozen and stabilized, the grenade would be detonated. An American sniper was summoned to shoot the Korean soldier in the head after his body had been placed—very carefully—in a vacant field. I did not witness the final chapter of this story, but I was told that the sharpshooter was reluctant to shoot a dead man in the head. The sharpshooter apparently missed the patient's head, and hit the nearby dirt instead. This jarring movement of the bullet's impact nearby caused the grenade to explode. The remains were given back to the Koreans and our problem was solved.

Not long after this sad incident, the Koreans invited me out to view their new hospital. The hospital was not yet fully operational, but most of the facilities were in place and the Korean doctors were quite proud of it. As I had helped several of the Korean doctors care for patients with neurological problems, I was one of the first American doctors invited to inspect the new Korean facility. I got in my jeep with a Korean physician, Dr. Shin, who was a psychiatrist. Dr. Shin was going to give me a private tour of the new facility, which was about six miles north of Nha Trang.

When we arrived at the guard gate, a guard stepped in front of my jeep with his rifle held in a smart salute. I waved at him and drove on by. Dr. Shin screamed in my ear, "Stop, stop, stop!" I asked why and he replied, "Just stop!" I stopped and looked back to see a nervous and shaky guard leveling his rifle at my head. Dr. Shin told me to back up as fast as I could which I promptly did. As it turned out, that guard had orders to shoot anyone who drove by without giving the password for the day. Dr. Shin gave him the password much to the relief of the guard. I asked Dr. Shin if the guard would have really shot me and he said, "Probably yes." Although the guard would not have wanted to shoot an American officer, he could have been court marshaled and put before a firing squad for disobeying orders. The Koreans are strict about orders. So we proceeded on toward the hospital compound.

Before we approached the compound, I noticed a small building on the side of a mountain. I asked, "What is that building and why is it there?" Dr. Shin told me that I was looking at the chapel. I said, "How can you get to it?" He replied, "It doesn't matter. No one goes there anyway." I thought to myself that this is right out of *Catch 22*.

We finally arrived at the hospital compound. It was nicely set up with hospital wards, operating rooms, recovery rooms, and everything we had in our hospital. We went to the perimeter of the hospital, which had many small huts built low to the ground much like tool sheds that one would see in America. I asked what the huts were used for and Dr. Shin told me it was where the corpsmen lived. The huts were strategically placed so the corpsmen could provide perimeter defense. I wanted to see a hut so Dr. Shin took me to visit one.

While Dr. Shin was talking to another officer, I decided to get a panoramic picture of the whole compound from the top of the hill. On my way to the top, I noticed several signs written in Korean and Vietnamese. I ignored the signs and continued walking up the hill. At the top I had a great view of the compound on one side of the hill, and a quaint Vietnamese village way down in the valley on the other side. I took some great pictures.

As I started to walk back down the hill, Dr. Shin hollered up to me, "Be pleased to come down the same way you went up." I asked why. He told me that I had just walked through a minefield. I replied, "Well then, I'm not coming down. You need to come get me." Dr Shin replied "Not to worry, my colleagues tell me there are not too many mines." I had no intention of moving and I asked Dr. Shin to call the American base and have a helicopter sent to pick me up. He said, "That will not make them happy." I replied, "I don't care. I'm not moving." About half an hour later, a helicopter came and picked me up and took me back to Nha Trang. As it turned out, the signs that I had disregarded were signs that said, "Do not proceed: Area is mined." When I got back to base at the 8th Field Hospital, I was told that I could have diverted a helicopter from bringing in real casualties and therefore I was told not to leave the base for the next two months. Looking back on this incident, I see it as a day where I could have been killed through ignorance and stupidity. I vowed never to repeat that again.

THE SUBSTITUTE BOYFRIEND

*A*s a neurologist, I had some unusual patients. One patient, a young lady in her 20's, was brought into the hospital by the CIA to be seen because of severe migraine headaches. She was a gorgeous, young Eurasian—half-French and half-Vietnamese—woman who worked for the CIA in the local bars and clubs. Her job was to obtain information from the American soldiers. The CIA figured that a female working for the Viet Cong or "the other side" was the perfect information gatherer. I learned that my patient came from an upper middle class family and did not want to be considered the same as the "B-girls" (bar girls) who were basically prostitutes. I found her to be charming and likable. I prescribed Fiorinal for her migraines, which, on a follow-up visit, I learned worked well to relieve her migraine pain. That was the last I saw of her except for a renewal prescription that was requested by the CIA officer a few months later.

About three weeks after I last heard from her, an enlisted man told me, "You're a real fox, Captain Carr. I have to give you credit." I had no idea what he was talking about but the comments kept coming from multiple people. After hearing these comments for about three weeks, I cornered one of the enlisted men to learn what was behind them. He told me, "The girl you are living with is a real knock out." I said, "What girl?" He described the young Eurasian patient I had treated for migraines. It turned out that she apparently was using me to rebuff the soldiers' unwanted attention. She was telling people that Captain Carr was her "man" and he would not approve of her having a relationship with anyone else. As soon as enlisted men heard that she was with an officer, they would leave her alone. It apparently helped her a lot and it certainly did not hurt my reputation either; but I never saw her again.

1966 Tent City

1966 Nha Trang Beach

1966 "The Beer Vendor"

1966 "Nung Guards", Pan & Lu

1966 "The Koreans" – Physicians

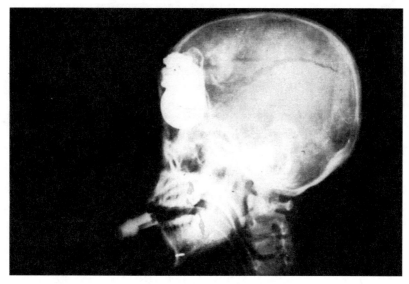

1966 "The Koreans": Grenade in Head

1966 "The Koreans" Mined Hill

1966 The Province Hospital

1966 After "The Ball Game"

2004: A Montagnard (Cham tribe)

2004: Nha Trang

2004: Remnants of war at Cu Chi

THE MISSIONARY FAMILY

*A*t the 8th Field Hospital in Nha Trang, I met a Red Cross worker, a young woman around the age of 25. Her role was to give out "comfort kits" containing toothbrushes, toothpaste, combs, hand mirrors, sewing kits, razor blades, soap, and a small bottle of after-shave lotion. She also wrote letters for wounded soldiers who could not write. She became friendly with a missionary who had a church and a home north of town on the top of a small hill with a beautiful view of the South China Sea.

At Christmas time the missionary wanted to invite four or five of the Army personnel to his home to share the holiday. Since I was a friend of the Red Cross woman, she asked me to go with her, and she asked me to invite three of my friends who would enjoy this excursion. Theoretically, the missionary's home and church were off limits for military personnel because they were located off base and outside of town, making it outside of the U.S. defenses. But things were quiet at the moment and the missionary never had problems with the Viet Cong, so I figured it was a safe place to have Christmas dinner.

The Red Cross woman knew the way to the missionary's home so we all got in my jeep and proceeded on our way to an old-fashioned, family Christmas dinner. The missionary and his wife had two children, an eight-year-old boy, and a little girl, age five. The children were home for the holidays; they spent most of the year in a boarding school in Kuala Lumpur, Malaysia, as it was considered too dangerous to have them in Vietnam.

Our host's home was on top of a hill surrounded by large and lush Poinsettia plants. We had a delicious turkey dinner with all the trimmings, and an enjoyable afternoon. I was quite taken with the little girl and she seemed to like me a lot. She was the same age as my daughter, Christina, which made me feel especially close to her. I asked the missionary if I could visit them again since we had to leave before it got dark. He said, "that would be fine, and you could take my daughter to the beach since she loves it and we don't have time to take her."

I paid another visit the following Sunday, just before the kids had to return to Kuala Lumpur. The little girl and I had fun on the beach gathering exotic seashells and bargaining for tropical fruit that was sold by local vendors. I was completely fascinated by this little girl's ability to bargain in the Vietnamese language, which she spoke fluently. She obtained the fruit at half the price I was going to pay. This little five-year-old told me it was no fun if you didn't bargain! It was a memorable afternoon.

After I left Vietnam and was transferred to Letterman General Hospital in San Francisco, a fellow officer told me a tragic story. I learned that the missionary and his wife were killed, and their home and church were burned down during the Tet offensive. Luckily, both the children were in Kuala Lumpur at the time. I was never able to confirm this rumor, but it always makes me sad to think about it since the two days I spent with this lovely, caring family were among my favorite Vietnam memories.

THE BEER VENDOR

Shortly after I arrived in Vietnam, I noticed a field with a huge stack of cardboard containers held together by metal straps. The containers were stacked 20 feet high and about 30 feet wide on each side with barbed wire around them. I asked another officer who had been around for awhile about the container's content. He said, "you're looking at lots of beer, my friend." Apparently it was beer meant for the whole of Vietnam, but the ship had to unload the entire supply in Nha Trang because of mechanical problems with the ship. The beer was never distributed as planned.

With the rain and humid weather, the straps were starting to break and the beer cans were falling out in great piles. Rather than let it go to waste, the powers that be decided to give the beer away. On a designated day and hour, the gates surrounding this pile of beer were opened. Unfortunately, the soldiers started drinking the beer rather than taking it away to distribute it elsewhere. This activity caused a near riot because the soldiers were getting drunk. The military police came to clear out the area and to set up a more orderly manner of distributing the beer.

To manage this dilemma, a command decision was made by the military police. Ten soldiers at a time were allowed to purchase beer at 2 ½ cents per can with a minimum of one case with the stipulation that there was no drinking on the premises. I gladly partook of this windfall and gathered my money and stood in line to make my purchase. Being the scientist that I am, I also came armed with a bucket of water so I could drop a can of beer in the water. If the can floated high on the water, or if the can bubbled when held under water, I threw it away because it was no longer good. If the beer can barely floated, it was deemed salvageable and I kept it. After making several trips, and spending a minimal amount of money, I had several months' supply of refreshing beer to enjoy. The only sad part was watching the huge beer supply gradually diminish and knowing we probably would never see another supply come our way again.

THE SMELLS OF VIETNAM

*I*t is said that certain smells can trigger memory more than vision or hearing. I believe this is true because there are certain smells in Vietnam that were unique. When I walked to the 8th Field Hospital, I would pass the diesel generators that were used to supply power to the hospital. To this day, when I smell diesel exhaust fumes, memory of that walk to the hospital comes to mind.

Other smells were more unique. The Vietnamese would frequently save their garbage and put it outside their home. A small child, with a pig in a harness, would walk by and let the pig select his dinner from the garbage. Thus the pig would have his dinner while ridding the village of some of its garbage. However, the smell was distinctly unpleasant. In the evening smells became quite delightful at times, since most of the villagers' cooking was done over jungle hard wood charcoal, which, for me, was an extremely pleasant smell. The Vietnamese food and charcoal smoke mixed together was like a restaurant burning incense.

Other smells were less pleasant. When causalities were brought into the hospital you could almost tell what kind of wounds the injured had based on the smell. Great amounts of blood produced a sweet, sickly smell. If a body cavity was penetrated, it produced a different unpleasant smell. These smells were always coupled with the smell of wet and mildewed clothing. A lack of recent bathing added to these other smells produced something I've only experienced once since leaving Viet Nam. This event occurred when I treated an emergency room patient who had been in a severe automobile accident. The minute I started treating him, I found myself transported back to Vietnam because of the smell.

There were several other smells that are hard to describe, but distinctive. For example, there was the burning of the latrines' outputs (local night soil or feces) which the local farmers collected. I also remember the pleasant smell of burning incense at the Buddhist monasteries. I love the smell of incense and continue to occasionally burn it in my home today. There was also a delicacy called Nuoc-mam, which is made by fermenting fish. Fish parts such as heads and other inedible parts are placed in a crock. A round ceramic plate with holes is placed between layers of these fish parts, which allow the substance to slowly ferment. A fluid drips from the bottom of the crock and Nuoc-mam is created. This sauce is placed on rice and it is delicious, but I imagine you'd have to like anchovies to appreciate the taste. The smell is strong and unpleasant to most people and if you spill it on your hands, it is difficult to wash the smell off. But Nuoc-mam is high in protein and sometimes it is the only protein served at a meal. I liked it so much I was going to bring some home, but decided not to, because if the bottle ever broke in my trunk, both my trunk and I would be thrown off the airplane.

THE MONTAGNARDS

*M*ontagnards is a French name that refers to all the ethnic groups that live in the central mountain highlands of Vietnam. There are many different ethnic groups of Montagnards. The Vietnamese refer to them as Moie, which translates to "savage." The Montagnards are primitive people who live in communal houses. They were barely out of the Stone Age, as their tools were mostly wooden and they hunted with crossbows with no metal parts. The arrows were made of bamboo and folded leaves. The strings on the crossbows were either braided vines or strips of bamboo. At the time, the Vietnamese treated them as sub-human beings.

The American Green Berets recruited them to act as guides and guerrilla troops to fight against the Viet Cong and North Vietnamese. The Montagnards had no love for any Vietnamese. Their language was as different from Vietnamese as English is from Greek. Their religion was animistic which means that everything has a spirit. They live in separate tribes and the one I was most familiar with, the Rade, lived near Buon Ma Thuot. Because the Vietnamese would have nothing to do with them when they were sick or wounded, the Green Berets would bring them to our hospital.

Montagnards had no written language. The reason for this is an interesting story that a missionary friend of mine relayed to me. Apparently many years ago, when a French missionary tried to get the Montagnards to accept a written language, he was told they would not accept a written language because of the following legend.

Many, many years ago, shortly after the world began, the people of the world were separated and the supreme God said he would give each group a written language. To receive their written language the tribes would climb to the top of Dragon Mountain, which is one of the highest in central Vietnam, and bring something for God to write their language on. At the appointed time, all the people of the world—and to the Montagnards that was Vietnam—climbed the mountain and carried dry leaves or wood from trees to have their language written on it. One tribe of Montagnards, the Rade, were proud people and felt themselves superior to all others. They brought a greater material, buffalo skin, on which to have their language inscribed and they made fun of the lessor materials. God was not particular about the material and he wrote a language on whatever people brought. The Rade were to carry the language back to their people so they would have a written language.

On the way back to their home after receiving their written language, a tiger attacked the Rade. By the time they could catch up with the tiger, he had eaten the buffalo skin and their written language. The Rade returned to Dragon Mountain to ask God to give them their language again. God refused because he felt they were too proud and acted superior to their fellow man. Legend tells us that today's Rade refuse to accept a written language because of their ancestors' pride and vanity.

There is a second interesting legend about the Montagnard origin. Shortly after the world began, there was a great flood. At that time, the Montagnards lived far to the east of Vietnam and when the great flood overcame their homeland they built rafts and sailed west, landing on top of Dragon mountain where only the tip of the mountain was showing. As the floodwaters receded, the Montagnards went down the mountain and scattered in all directions, forming the various tribes of their world. This legend predates any exposure to Christianity and Noah's biblical flood. Archaeologists and anthropologists believe that these people, through language similarities and physical characteristics, probably did come from Polynesia although it had to have been many, many years ago. At one time the Montagnards, occupied and ruled most of Vietnam. Being invaded by the more advanced and better-equipped oriental race, they were gradually forced to the infertile and inhospitable central highlands, whereas most of the Vietnamese lived within 100 miles of the coast or in the extremely fertile rice-producing area of the Mekong Delta.

I have no pictures of Montagnards because they did not allow photographs to be taken. This practice is because they fear that taking their picture takes away part of their spirit. They had many other fears and superstitions which made them difficult to treat as patients. One fear was that if a person died away from the village, his or her spirit would wander through eternity trying to find the way home. This was a problem when treating a seriously ill Montagnard because if the family thought a loved one was going to die, they would remove all the IV's, life support, and medications and take the patient back home as quickly as possible. This action would allow the loved one a chance to die in their village where "he or she belonged." This practice was particularly frustrating when treating children because at times we were convinced that we could have saved the child. Sadly, the Montagnards were accustomed to their children dying as a matter of course. There was almost a 50% infant mortality in the child's first year of life. One of the Montagnards' beliefs was that a child should select his or her own name. Therefore they did not name a child until after one year. Families lived in a communal house and family members watched the child's behavior. If the child seemed attracted to certain people or people's possessions, the child would often be named after that person. From a sociological point of view, it was probably a defense mechanism because of the high infant mortality rate and, I guess, it would be easier to accept a child's death if he or she remained unnamed.

When the Montagnards were brought into an American hospital, the cultural diversity was huge. At times it was humorous; such as when a Rade, one tribe of Montagnards, could not figure how to open a door since he had never before seen a doorknob. When he saw the toilet, he had no idea what to do with it. I watched him put one foot on each side of the toilet seat and squat over it, which was similar to using a primitive slit trench. I recall a Red Cross volunteer giving a Rade a comfort kit. This kit consisted of toothpaste, comb, razor, and after-shave lotion. He had no idea what to do with the supplies. I saw another Rade using two toothbrushes as chopsticks to eat his lunch. The razor blades were their most prized possession. After a few minor cuts, they learned they were excellent tools to be used in the manufacture of their crossbows and arrows.

On one occasion I was called to see a Rade and I found him in a deep coma for no apparent reason. He came in with a high fever, probably from malaria, but after admission, he became completely unresponsive. I was asked to evaluate him to see if he had cerebral malaria. Upon examination, I noticed he had no papilledema that would indicate increased brain pressure and, what was more surprising, he had absent reflexes that are usually increased with cerebral malaria. His plantar reflexes were unresponsive and he did not respond to pain of any type. When the Internist asked me to diagnosis the condition, I replied, "I have no idea but I feel I should do a spinal tap." I did the spinal tap without the use of local anesthetic since he was not responding to pain. The spinal fluid was normal. At this point, I was completely baffled. The patient was found to have malaria and was treated for it. Two days later he suddenly woke up and was perfectly normal. He had a completely normal neurological exam including plantar responses. I later learned through an interpreter that when a Rade gets sick to the point of feeling he might die, he put himself into a trance, which is a common treatment among the Montagnards. The reason was that if he could fool the evil spirits that were causing his illness into thinking he was dead, these evil spirits would leave him and he would return to good health. It was hard for me to believe that a person could put himself into such a deep trance that he was unresponsive to everything including absent reflexes, but that seems to be what had happened. This patient subsequently made a full recovery and returned to his village. My time learning about the Montagnard culture was a fascinating part of my Vietnam experience.

THE GRAVE DETAIL

One of the least pleasant tasks that befell the officers of the 8th Field Hospital was what we referred to as the grave detail. This task consisted of going to the morgue and making out death certificates for those killed in action (KIA). The officers performed grave detail on a rotation basis. For that reason, it was not often that we had to do this odious task.

The first time I was requested to perform my duty, the first dead soldier I encountered was one who had been incinerated by Napalm. When I viewed the body, even though it was completely unrecognizable, the morgue attendant said I had to examine the body to determine the exact cause of death so I could complete the death certificate. Having never seen an incinerated person before, viewing the remains left me feeling nauseous and faint. I said, "It is obvious what killed him. He was burned to death." The attendant replied, "No, it makes a difference if he was killed before he was incinerated or after." I asked, "How could I possibly tell that?" The attendant suggested we x-ray the patient. X-ray results revealed multiple fragment wounds in the brain and throughout his chest, abdomen and limbs. I decided that the cause of death was likely due to fragments and the incineration came later. This was an important distinction since the soldier was in a fire fight with the Viet Cong and was noted to be wounded or killed as the soldiers were withdrawing from the field and air support was called in to drop Napalm on the advancing Viet Cong. This action stopped the enemy from advancing, but it led to the incineration of this already dead soldier. It made a difference whether we napalmed our own live soldiers or those who were already KIA.

There were three times I almost fainted while serving as a physician in Vietnam. The first time was seeing the incinerated soldier. The second time was when I was a triage officer and casualties were brought in. This one soldier was lying on a stretcher and he was covered with a blanket. He asked me if I would move his leg because it was uncomfortable and giving him pain. I turned his foot with the boot on, and found out that it was completely severed from his leg. Because it was so unexpected and because the patient was unaware of it, I started feeling light headed. The third time I nearly fainted was when a patient came in face down on a canvas stretcher, and his face was in a pool of blood. I needed to move him to a gurney and asked him if he could roll over. He said he would, but his speech was garbled and almost unintelligible. When he rolled over, the lower part of his face stuck to the canvas stretcher as he had been shot through both sides of his lower jaw. Again, because I did not expect it, I experienced a sudden emotional jolt. Other than these three incidences, I held up quite well to horrors of war casualties.

Grave detail was unpleasant, as the wounds were often quite gruesome such as decapitations, disembowelments, etc. I found that when I was called to perform grave detail, if I drank a certain amount of Vodka prior to going to the morgue, I could complete the task much easier. Luckily, I did not have to do the job more than four times during the year I spent in Vietnam.

ALCOHOL IN VIETNAM

*A*lcoholism was a problem for American troops in Vietnam although the Army tended to deny it. My KO unit was made up primarily of psychiatrists, psychologists, and social workers. The team confirmed that alcoholism was indeed a problem because they saw a number of patients who were suffering from it. Alcohol was readily available and inexpensive, and, while in Vietnam, soldiers did not have to pay taxes on it. I was surprised to learn how much various taxes such as federal, state, and local add to the cost of a bottle of alcohol. Without these taxes, a bottle of Scotch would cost somewhere between three to six dollars a bottle.

The CO of our unit proposed to the area commander that he would like to start an Alcoholic Anonymous (AA) program in order to try and control the problem. The area commander told our CO that the Army did not have a problem with alcohol and therefore an AA program was not needed in Vietnam. End of subject.

Not only was alcohol a problem to some of those soldiers who consumed it, but it also led to dangerous and sometimes deadly encounters. One incident involved a group of men who were drinking and gambling. One GI accused another GI of cheating. Both were drunk and they decided to settle it "the old western way." They started shooting at each other with their side arms, resulting in the death of one and the wounding of the other. This type of incident was not uncommon. Sometimes the weapon used would be a 45 caliber, other times an M16 or a grenade. At one time, such types of "friendly fire" caused one fourth of the casualties we had in the hospital. This behavior was not unexpected when you consider that a number of GI's were there because a judge back in the States gave them a choice between enlisting in the Army or doing jail time for some felony they had committed. At times, these hostile and psychopathic personalities made good soldiers; at other times, especially when drunk, they were quite dangerous.

Smoking marijuana was also prevalent and company commanders usually regarded it as being preferable to drinking. Smoking marijuana did not seem to cause the anger and hostility that resulted from consuming too much alcohol. The other preference for marijuana over alcohol was that in an emergency, such as an attack, the pot smokers seemed to respond in a more appropriate manner than a drunken soldier. In either case, the Army ignored the problems associated with chemical dependency.

Drinking was a problem among the officers in support areas, as well as the enlisted men—with the exception of combat officers. These were soldiers in Vietnam who were doing their "hardship tour" prior to retiring and did not volunteer or really didn't want to be in Vietnam. The officers tended to have more medical problems related to the alcohol than the enlisted men. Problems included peripheral neuropathy, cerebella ataxia, and tremor. The likely reason for this was that the enlisted men were provided food and had to show up for "mess" or they would be in trouble. The officers, on the other hand, were completely on their own to decide whether they ate or not, and officers had to pay for their food. Most people who drink heavily tend to neglect eating. It is my feeling that many of the medical complications from alcohol are as much from malnutrition as the alcohol itself.

The class six store where alcohol was sold was located at MACV (Military Assistance Command Vietnam), which was an enclosed, walled-in area with several buildings in the downtown area of Nha Trang. Included in these buildings were a movie theater and a liquor store. One day, one of the neurosurgeons and I decided we needed to replenish our supply of Scotch. We found a private who was delivering something to the MACV complex and we asked for a ride to the liquor store. He readily agreed, and we went and bought our Scotch. My colleague bought the more expensive Johnny Walker black label, and I bought the cheaper Johnny Walker red. I said, "Why pay more when you can get the red label?" He replied, "Because the black label is better." I told him I doubted he could tell the difference. As we were driving back to the 8th Field Hospital compound, we continued our argument. About halfway home, we had to stop to let a water buffalo cross the road in front of us. Our driver could not get the jeep to restart, and my colleague and I were in no condition to help. The driver started walking back to the USO center to call for help from the motor pool while we waited in the jeep.

While the driver was away, our disagreement about the better Scotch escalated to the point where we decided to have a little contest. We closed our eyes and alternately took a swig from each bottle in the attempt to differentiate the black from the red label. My colleague was correct the first time, I guessed wrong, and we both agreed that this contest could be simply chance. So we decided to try two out of three tests. The second round we both got it right, but I felt it was still just chance. The third time we both got it wrong. By this time, neither one of us remembered just how much Scotch we had drunk. Shortly thereafter, the private returned and was surprised to find us drunk. He looked at us in a disapproving manner, probably thinking that we, as medical officers, should not be drinking so much. Of course he didn't say anything to us because he was a private and we were captains. A moment later, the mechanic from the motor pool arrived, got in the jeep, turned the key, and the jeep started up immediately. He looked at our driver, two drunken officers, shook his head, muttered something inaudible and left us. By the time we got to base and to our villa, we were pretty much wasted. We had consumed about half of the alcohol we had purchased.

MY VIETNAM RELIGIOUS EXPERIENCE

*P*eople close to me know that I am not a religious person. War has a way of changing people, and shortly after I arrived in Vietnam, and without much to do on Sundays, I decided to give church a try. Besides, I figured it was not a bad idea to practice some faith considering the living environment I was temporarily calling home.

The Protestant minister held services in part of the mess hall on Sunday mornings. I went to the service one time, and I did not particularly care for the sermon, but the socializing with the nurses and other doctors was nice. The minister, however, was unhappy and depressed about being in Vietnam. He was trying every possible means to get a medical diagnosis that would send him back home. He asked me on a few occasions what neurological diagnoses would get him sent back to the States. I told him there weren't many. My short list consisted of a brain tumor, multiple sclerosis, or Parkinson's disease. He asked me about headaches. I told him that everyone in Vietnam had headaches—including me. I offered to prescribe some medicine called Fiorinal. He was not happy with my suggestion and continued his inquires with other medical specialists. Soon after this conversation, the minister received a letter from his wife stating that she was having severe pain from a condition called endometriosis—a female condition that causes severe abdominal pain. The minister consulted with a general surgeon who was an OB-GYN specialist back in the States. The minister asked what could be done to treat this condition. The physician enjoyed replying, "If she got pregnant, the symptoms would disappear." With this treatment in mind, the minister somehow persuaded the powers that be that he had to be reassigned back to the States in order to treat his wife's endometriosis.

This minister was in such a hurry to leave that he taped a sermon that was to be delivered on Thanksgiving Day two days hence. We all assembled for our Thanksgiving services, and sitting on the pulpit was a tape recorder. One of the minister's assistants started it, and that was to be our sermon for the day. I was not too impressed with the minister previously, and I was less impressed with him now.

Next, I decided to give Catholicism a try. Our priest was an amiable fellow but he had one fault: he liked to drink alcohol. On a typical Saturday night, you could find at least one party to attend and it was the priest's habit not to miss this social opportunity. On Sunday morning, the priest would often have a hangover that made his sermons less than exciting. In fact, they were abbreviated and delivered without a great deal of enthusiasm. I quickly lost interest in the Catholic faith.

During dinner one evening, I overheard one of our neurosurgeons, Dr. Blum, talking about how disappointed the local itinerant Rabbi was because they did not have enough men to hold a proper Jewish service. I learned that ten men needed to be present to conduct the service— women did not count—and the group was one man short of this meeting requirement. I quickly offered to attend the services, and, after attending it, I found it to be quite enjoyable. I liked the sermon and the music. For the next few months, I would put on the yarmulke and take my place as the tenth man during the service. It was not until sometime later that I learned I did not really count as the tenth man because I was not Jewish. I asked Dr. Blum why he did not tell me this fact. He replied, "You seemed so happy to be helping the other Jewish men out that I didn't want to disappoint you." I continued to attend services anyway. In some respects, Jewish services were not that different from the Unitarian church that I attended as a child.

I never developed an affinity for religion, but I gained a certain level of confidence that helped me live in the war zone. After attending all three churches, I felt that in the likelihood of an attack by the enemy, I had all the bases covered for the afterlife.

THE BALL GAME

*A*fter being in Vietnam for several months, the CO of our unit felt that the morale was somewhat low mostly due to the working conditions in Camp McDermott, or "Tent City," where the psychiatrists and the enlisted men worked. As a morale booster, the CO decided that a softball game would be scheduled that would pit the enlisted men against the officers.

With a lot of fanfare, a game was arranged. As there were only seven officers in our team, we enlisted two other medical officers. We selected them on the basis that they would add some athletic prowess to our pitiful, non-athletic team. The game was widely advertised which counted for the number of fans who arrived to witness this special event.

I am not considered much of an athlete. I am not skilled at either catching or throwing a ball. This skill deficiency made it difficult for the team to decide where to place me on the field. Knowing I had to play somewhere, I was relegated to the right field position. The officers were up first and we quickly registered three strikeouts. The enlisted men fared better when they scored six runs the first time up at bat.

During the second inning, I got to hit the ball and I actually made it to first base. Sadly, I remained there for the rest of the inning. And so it went until the score in the 6th inning was 14–0. By this time I had become discouraged, and when I was out in right field, I decided to go to the sidelines and enjoy a beer with the nurses. While there, as fate would have it, a ball was hit into right field. As I was sitting on the sidelines drinking beer, I was not there to catch it. Having missed at least six balls previously and having made errors in throwing that allowed home runs for the enlisted men, I felt this was no great problem. My team had a different attitude. As luck would have it, we got a break. Once it was found that there was no right fielder on the field, the umpire decided to call the hit as a ground rule double.

When I returned to the field, I actually caught the next ball that was hit, thus, ending the inning. As it turned out, my best play of the game was to be sitting on the sidelines, drinking a beer with the nurses. Our CO said the game was a great morale booster for the enlisted men under his command. He thanked me for adding some humor to the game and told me I could play on his team in the right field position any time.

CLOTHING & JEWELRY

*B*efore going to Vietnam, I was told not to bring any light-colored clothing including underwear, socks, tee shirts, and even the insignia sewn on our fatigue uniforms. I was told this was a rule because light-colored clothing would make a soldier a good target for the enemy. We also were not allowed to bring anything shiny such as wristwatches, wedding rings, or anything else that would disclose our location in a combat situation. Because of the heat and humidity in Vietnam, I was told to convert from using the brief-type underwear to the boxer type. As most men know, boxer underwear offers looseness and more circulation so wearers are less likely to get rashes and fungus infections. Having never worn boxer underwear, this practice was not to my liking as I was uncomfortable without the additional support. Although I did buy some boxer shorts, I made sure I had a good supply of my Jockey briefs because I wore them anyway.

On a designated day I was required to have all my light colored clothing labeled with my name and left in a certain area where it would be picked up and dyed olive green by a special platoon of enlisted men. My newly dyed clothing would be returned to me and this supply would become my wardrobe during my tour of duty in Vietnam.

In looking back, I realized that where I was stationed, dyeing my underwear and other clothing items was definitely not necessary. This was because I was not in combat, my underwear never showed, and I was never too close to sniper fire. But I had to remember that while in the Army, orders are orders and I had to obey them even if they did not make sense to me.

As far as jewelry was concerned, I left my wedding ring at home with my wife, and the Army issued me a special combat watch to wear instead of my favorite gold watch with an expandable wristband. I was told that the combat watch was an excellent watch and it was waterproof. It had a black wristband and numbers that faintly glowed in the dark. The style of this watch looked like WWII surplus. After arriving in Vietnam, I wore the watch when I went swimming. When I came out of the water, it was completely full of water, with a small bubble on top of the crystal; so much for the waterproof guarantee. The only use I could make of it was as a level. Since it was the only watch I had, I was determined to salvage it. I drilled a small hole in the crystal, which was plastic, and drained the water out the best I could. I rinsed it several times with acetone trying to dry it completely. This process dried the watch to the point where it started working again, but the acetone removed all of the numbers so I had to guess at the time. This was not too difficult because one can guess pretty closely where the numbers belong. The watch worked quite well but I never wore it in the shower or swimming again.

THE EXECUTED PATIENT

A few months after I arrived in Vietnam and settled into my neurology practice, I received orders that outlined the requirement for recording my patient examinations. The report required the patient's name, diagnosis, treatment, and final disposition—and it had to be typed. I was required to give a monthly report to my commanding officer who would sign and forward it to a senior officer in Saigon. The report, with all accompanying signatures, would end up in either the archive of the Pentagon or at Bethesda Medical Center. My intuition told me the reports were not being read because of the volume of recorded cases.

Our unit had a clerk typist who was located in Camp McDermott on the other side of the base. He was assigned to work with the psychiatrists. There was also a clerk typist at the 8th Field Hospital, but he was not in my chain of command so I could not order him to do the work. Thus, the typing became my responsibility. I managed to scrounge up an old typewriter and I proceeded to complete these reports by myself with the slow "two finger" approach. The process was laborious and time consuming.

About a month after I learned I was required to complete these reports, a sergeant brought in an unusual patient—an injured cat. The sergeant was given the job of taking care of three cats that belonged to a lieutenant. He was required to change the litter, feed them, etc. and he was not happy about the assignment. The sergeant did not like cats and resented this extra duty so he decided to play a practical joke on the lieutenant—running the cat up a wooden flagpole. The sergeant thought the cat would stay on top of the flagpole until the lieutenant came home that evening. The sergeant was looking forward to watching the lieutenant get upset over trying to figure out how to get the cat down safely.

As most everyone knows, cats can climb up trees and other similar surfaces, but they do not have the ability to climb back down because of the angle and positioning of their claws. This cat, however, lacked the natural instincts of most cats. Instead of waiting to be rescued, he jumped from the top of the pole. When the sergeant recovered the cat, he found it could not move its hind legs. In a panic, the sergeant brought the cat to the 8th Field Hospital to see what could be done for it.

At that time we had no veterinarian unit at the hospital and because the cat was paralyzed, it was deemed a neurological problem so I was called in to treat it. I confirmed that my patient was indeed paralyzed. X-rays confirmed my diagnosis of a broken back with a severed spinal cord. I told the sergeant, "There is nothing medically we can do for this cat. Euthanasia appears to be the only answer." No one was quite sure how to treat the cat in a pharmaceutical sense, but the sergeant was quite willing to solve the problem. He took the cat out behind the hospital and he shot it with his 45-caliber side arm. The lieutenant, who owned the cat, never did learn about the incident.

I thought about how I should document the cat incident and I decided to have some fun. In my monthly report I stated, "Patient was brought in with paralysis from mid-thoracic spine down; x-rays confirmed a severed spinal cord. The patient was taken behind the 8th Field Hospital and shot to death." I submitted this report as usual and it was signed off by my company commander, and forwarded to Saigon. Never being asked to explain the report confirmed my original supposition that the reports were not being read. I am sure to this day that you could find my report somewhere at the Pentagon or in Bethesda Medical Center. Maybe someday I will be asked to explain my drastic treatment course for this particular patient, but I doubt it.

CASUALTIES OF WAR

*U*nlike the television series *M*A*S*H,* the majority of our patients had medical illnesses that were not combat casualties. There were times when we did not see a combat casualty for weeks on end, but there were always medical patients. The conditions we treated most frequently were malaria, scrub typhus, dengue fever, and the other more common medical problems that one would see in a stateside hospital. I believe that part of the reason we did not see many casualties was that we were not in an area with the most active fighting. However, in talking with my colleagues in other hospitals throughout Vietnam, they confirmed that most of their patients were medical also.

When we did have casualties to treat we were often notified well in advance—and at a particular time. The Army had an uncanny ability to accurately predict how many casualties we would receive. For instance, if the Army was sending a company of troops against an estimated company of enemy, they could estimate very accurately the number of wounded and killed in action that we could expect to see.

It was interesting to watch the medevac helicopters lining up with the appropriate number of body bags just waiting for a call. Those of us working at medical facilities would receive a call before there were any injuries to tell us what we could expect. I learned how statistics played a key role in helping us anticipate casualties. For example, if soldiers were in a firefight between troops shooting each other, the Army could estimate that one in four of the casualties would be killed and three others would require medical attention. If the soldiers were going up against artillery or mortars, only one in ten would be killed and we could expect nine casualties to be treated at our hospital.

When casualties did arrive, I, as a Neurologist, was of little use as a treating physician so I was made a triage officer. My duty was to assess the casualties as they arrived and determine what immediate steps were required to treat the patient such as sending him to x-ray, type and cross-matching blood, or sending the patient to the pre-surgical area. On rare occasions the patient was placed on the "expectant list." The soldiers who were placed on this list were expected to die no matter what treatment was given to them. I can say that in my entire year in Vietnam, I only placed two patients on the expectant list. One was a patient with an intra-cranial rifle grenade injury; the other was a patient who was missing a great deal of bowel and other internal organs who lived for only 30 minutes after he arrived at the hospital. On the whole, if a trauma patient made it to the Field Hospital alive, he had a 99% survival rate. That statistic is better than any hospital in the states.

On one occasion, President Johnson traveled to Cam Ranh Bay to show his support of the boys fighting the war. His goal was to pin some Purple Heart medals on our patients. We were asked to send patients to meet President Johnson but we had such a paucity of battle casualties that we did not have enough patients to send him. There were none in Cam Ranh Bay since their medical facilities were primarily for Air Force and a malaria rehabilitation hospital. We had one severe casualty in the hospital, but he was too sick to send to Cam Ranh Bay just to receive a medal. We eventually found a patient who had actually shot himself accidentally practicing "quick draw" with his 45 and sent him to meet President Johnson. We also found two other patients who had sustained slight wounds during a local mortar attack to go with him. Although technically the person with the self-inflicted wound was not entitled to a Purple Heart medal, I do not think anyone took it away from him after having it presented to him by the President of the United States.

MILITARY COURTESY

*W*hen I was first drafted into the Army, I reported two days late for duty for personal reasons. Because of this absence, I missed my training on military courtesies. Missing this training came back to haunt me when I was in Saigon.

I had just toured the 17th Field Hospital in Saigon along with the commanding general, one colonel and a major. Following the tour, we were to be taken to a restaurant for dinner. The commanding officer ordered a car to take us there and when it arrived, I opened the back door and waited for the general to get in. The general immediately grabbed me by the back of the neck and shoved me into the car. I later learned from the major that there was a proper way to enter a car with other officers. First, the driver, who is an enlisted man, is supposed to open the door.

Then, the lowest ranking officer, who happened to be me, gets in first. The other officers then get into the car according to rank. Finally the highest-ranking officer gets in last. I felt I was being polite, but apparently I offended the general not knowing this basic military courtesy. I never did learn the rationale for this protocol.

I picked up most of the other military courtesies, as I went along without any other major confrontations. One exception occurred with the comedienne entertainer, Martha Ray. Ms. Ray was in Vietnam to entertain the troops. During an earlier visit, she was made an honorary colonel which included being given a new hat with the colonel insignia to wear. One evening, I passed her on my way to the 8th Field Hospital. She was on her way to perform a show. I glanced at her and said "Hello." She became indignant and asked why I didn't salute a superior officer. I replied, "I didn't see a superior officer." She pointed to the insignia on her hat and said, "You don't salute me, you salute the rank." I thought the whole incident was rather silly and she went off muttering something about me being court marshaled. I never cared much for Martha Ray before this incident and I cared less for her afterwards.

BLACK OPS

*A*fter I had been in Vietnam for six months, one of my patients, who was an officer, asked me if I could bring a few of the doctors and nurses to have dinner in a compound where he worked. I assumed it was a thank you gift for providing medical care to him. Always ready to get off the base and do something new, I readily accepted his invitation. I arranged for three nurses and four doctors to accompany me to dinner at this patient's compound. A driver picked us up at 6:00 P.M. sharp.

When we arrived at the compound, I noticed that it was completely walled in and it was located on the outskirts of Nha Trang. I noticed there was high security; armed guards were everywhere. I started having second thoughts about visiting this patient, but since we had already arrived, there was not much I could do about it.

It turned out that our hosts were American pilots who were kept isolated on this compound 24/7. They were happy to see some fellow Americans—especially the nurses. I asked one of the pilots what he did and he replied, "I fly airplanes." I sarcastically said, "I had guessed that you flew airplanes, but I was wondering where you fly and on what kind of missions." He replied that it was a secret and that response made me even more curious about his vocation.

Since I was not going to get any other information from him, I decided to let it go. My colleagues and I settled in to enjoy the drinks, dinner and companionship. I still remember the dinner as being one of the best meals I had in Vietnam.

As the evening wore on I never learned what these pilots did or where they flew. I did learn that they flew C130 cargo planes that were painted black and had no insignia, and I learned that they carried troops which were non-American, had Czech weapons and they flew to unknown destinations.

When we left the compound later that evening, we were told to say nothing of what we had heard or tell anyone where we had been. To my knowledge, none of us ever spoke of this interesting evening again. And we were never invited back.

As I reflect on that evening, I suspect these pilots probably worked for the CIA and they were most likely flying into Laos, Cambodia and perhaps even parachuting agents into North Vietnam, although that is my own speculation based on what I have learned since the war ended.

What I can say is that it was an enjoyable evening and the pilots seemed to have the best of everything in the way of liquor and food. I wonder how many of them made it back to America?

THE VIET CONG PUPPY

*I*n early 1967, one unit of the 25th infantry division was on a search and destroy mission in an area close to Nha Trang. The soldiers came across a small village that appeared to be abandoned. They set out to confirm this assumption, and to search for enemy contraband and weapons.

As the soldiers were searching one of the bamboo huts, they found an occupant: a scared puppy. One of the soldiers walked toward the puppy and, when he got close enough, the puppy made an aggressive move and bit the soldier on the leg. The bite didn't hurt much because the puppy was so small, and because the bite barely scratched the skin's surface. The soldier laughed because he thought it was funny to see such a little thing act so boldly. This incident triggered an idea that would allow him to have some fun with his buddies. He found an old blanket in the hut to wrap the puppy in; he scooped up the little animal, and left the hut.

The soldier brought the puppy into a different hut where one of his buddies was searching. He placed the animal on the ground, and released him from the blanket. The puppy quickly ran to the soldier who was searching the hut, and bit him on the leg. After the initial shock and anger wore off, both soldiers enjoyed a good laugh, and they colluded on ways to continue this game. They wrapped the puppy in the blanket once again, and took him back to their base camp. They named him VC puppy because of where they found him, and because of his aggressive nature.

When the two buddies got back to base camp, they released the puppy into a tent that contained four or five soldiers. As expected, the puppy acted quickly, and bit several of them. Everyone thought this scene was hilarious so they took the puppy to yet another tent to replay the game—and got the same results. When the fun and games were over, VC puppy had bitten a total of twelve soldiers.

Shortly after the game ended, one of the soldiers noted that VC puppy appeared tired and somewhat ill. The soldiers attributed this condition to the energy that the puppy used to fulfill his role in the game, and they felt guilty about exhausting the little guy. The next morning produced a real surprise: VC puppy had died sometime during the night.

The puppy's death turned merriment into worry. The soldiers brought the puppy's remains to the veterinarian hospital, which was attached to the 8th Field Hospital. The veterinarian hospital existed to treat and maintain a large contingency of guard dogs that were used to protect the facilities, and hunt down the Viet Cong. A veterinarian performed an autopsy on the puppy, and the soldiers nervously awaited the results. The pathology revealed intraneuronal inclusion bodies (Negri bodies) in the cerebellar Purkingee cells. Intrepretation: the puppy died of rabies.

Quickly, all twelve soldiers who VC puppy had bitten were summoned to the 8th Field Hospital for examination. The medical team noted that the animal bites were not severe; they were more like small puncture wounds. The local doctors told me that it is unusual for people to get rabies from rabid animals if the bites are minor such as those we saw inflicted by VC puppy. As a precaution for these twelve soldiers, however, each received the common treatment for rabies: a series of painful, duck embryo anti-serum injections that were administered directly into the abdominal wall.

Of interest, rabies is endemic in Southeast Asia, and it was not uncommon to see rabid dogs near the 8th Field Hospital. In my year stay in Nha Trang, I saw only two cases of human rabies. Both patients were Vietnamese children who were savagely bitten by rabid dogs on the face and neck, and both had died.

As I reflected on the incident involving the twelve soldiers, I think this puppy may have been left behind in the bamboo hut on purpose. Perhaps the Viet Cong used this rabid puppy as a vehicle for biological warfare—a little far-fetched, I'll admit, but within the realm of possibilities.

"THE SHELF"

*T*he USO would bring entertainment for the troops on occasion while I was stationed in Nha Trang. One such entertainer was a male magician. The magician's assistant was a young lady who wore a skimpy costume and was extremely well endowed.

After the first show, word got around about the magician's assistant and soldiers were rushing to watch her in the magic show. In fact, in all subsequent magic shows, it was standing room only. The troops were not enthusiastic about the magician; they just came to see the assistant who developed a pseudonym, "the shelf." In fact, at one point, they booed one of the magician's tricks because "the shelf" was not part of the act.

When the magician finished his gigs in Nha Trang and moved on to another destination, "the shelf" decided that there was money to be made in Nha Trang. She chose to stay on and she was determined to open her own nightclub in downtown Nha Trang where she would be the star performer. It was difficult to open an establishment of this type in a Vietnamese city because there were many licenses to obtain and many officials to bribe.

While "the shelf" was still performing with her magician, she lived in the nurses' quarters and became friendly with a nurse, Barbie, who was my friend. This is how I got to know what was happening with "the shelf."

After making her way through all the red tape, "the shelf" was finally going to have a grand opening of her club. To give her act an air of class and acceptability she wanted to have Americans, both male and female, attend the opening. My nurse friend Barbie asked me to escort her. As it turned out, "the shelf" did not have enough financial backing to pay off the required bribes after all, so the club never opened, and she moved on to some other place or perhaps she even joined up with the magician once again.

This story illustrates the difficulty, if not impossibility, of becoming an entrepreneur in Vietnam at that time unless you were a rich Vietnamese. I had to give her credit for trying.

SLEEPING ON THE JOB

In a combat area, all facilities are guarded day and night. Pulling guard duty is not usually the most favored duty because 99.9% of the time it is extremely boring. Since the guard is the first line of defense and he or she is responsible for alerting the unit of impending danger, this position is highly regarded by military leaders. In fact, being caught sleeping on guard duty is considered a serious offense that is punishable by a lengthy prison term or, in time of major conflict, by death.

When a person is arrested for sleeping on guard duty, it leads to a court marshal. In the legal world, most JAG officers knew of only one legitimate defense for this crime: narcolepsy. This is a medical condition that occurs when a patient goes into normal sleep at unusual times and is unable to stay awake. The patient will often drift off to sleep at inappropriate times. As a neurologist, this is where I came into the picture. JAG lawyers would bring an offender to the hospital to be evaluated for narcolepsy.

In order to diagnose this disease, I look for a long history of problems staying awake plus a characteristic EEG (electroencephalogram) pattern showing abnormal REM (rapid eye movement) sleep. Since no EEG equipment was available in Vietnam, I relied on the patient's oral history.

After my first couple of patients, I noticed a trend with the narcolepsy patients I evaluated. By the time most of them reached me, they seemed to be well versed in how to provide an appropriate history, so I could do little but diagnose narcolepsy. I knew that if I challenged the facts and did not diagnose narcolepsy, the soldiers might spend ten years in Leavenworth. Once a soldier was diagnosed with narcolepsy, he was given a medical profile that assigned him to duty where the condition would not be a hazard to either himself or to others.

Of course, you and I know that some of these diagnoses were not valid which is a fact that both patient and commanders realized. I recalled one such patient who ended up being a driver for the commanding general. I thought that was an interesting reassignment for someone who could not stay awake.

AN UNUSUAL CASE

*T*he 8th Field Hospital where I worked received a call to inform us that casualties were being brought in. One of the casualties was a man who was in a coma without signs of other injury. I was alerted to be in the triage area to evaluate the comatose patient.

When the patient arrived at the hospital, several other casualties that were injured in the same mortar attack accompanied him. One of the injured men told me that my patient was ducking for cover when the mortar attack began. The patient suddenly fell to the ground following one of the mortar explosions and he never moved until the attack was finally repulsed, which was eight to twelve hours later. Everyone thought my patient was dead, but when they went to recover the body, they found he was still breathing. That was when he was brought to the hospital for treatment.

Upon examination, I found the patient to have severe papilledema, which indicates severe increased intracranial pressure, but he had no obvious head injuries. I looked over his body and found what looked like a small fragment entry area on his chest, but it was tiny. He was also covered with scrapes and old leech bites and it was hard for me to tell if this was a wound or not. A chest x-rayed revealed no metal fragments. I called the neurosurgeons to put in burr holes looking for evidence of subdural bleeding. They found no evidence of bleeding, but the brain was under tremendous pressure from generalized swelling. The patient was hospitalized and after approximately ten hours, he died.

At post mortem he was found to have a punctured heart and he had bled into the pericardial cavity causing a cardiac compression, which probably caused his final demise, although he would have certainly died from his severe brain swelling in any event. We were baffled by what had punctured his heart so we x-rayed his entire body and found a small metal fragment lodged in his femoral artery at the bifurcation.

Piecing together what had happened, we surmised that the fragment had penetrated his chest and traveled into his heart, which probably caused a cardiac arrest, which resulted in severe anoxic brain swelling. Then, sometime shortly thereafter, the heart began pumping again and pumped the metal fragment out of the heart to its final destination—his leg, which is why we missed it upon examination of the chest. This case produced the most unusual sequence of events, but that is the only way we could explain the findings of this soldier's unfortunate and mysterious death.

THE SHORT TIMER

When a soldier's tour of duty in Vietnam is almost over, Army personnel label him a "short timer." Soldiers—especially those in combat—have a terrible fear of getting wounded or killed during the last few days before they are scheduled to leave the country and return home to the United States. So when someone is designated as a "short timer" it is an emotional time for him.

To identify someone's "short timer" status, a soldier carries a special stick that is similar to a swagger stick. This stick usually has either knobs or a series of notches that identify the number of days you have left in country. When someone carries this stick, a couple of things happen. First, the soldier receives a lot of congratulations from his buddies for surviving the past year. Second, as a special bonus, "short timers" do not get any new dangerous assignments. It is like getting a paid vacation—on the clock. The "short timer" stick is not as significant for the doctors since we were rarely in combat danger.

When a "short timer" was scheduled to leave Vietnam, he was flown down to a replacement facility and was processed out of country in much the same way as when he left the United States the previous year. For example, each soldier was required to get a haircut, have clean uniforms, make sure his boots were polished etc. It was rumored that if a soldier did not pass inspection, he was denied boarding rights for his flight home. I am not sure why we were told to look our best for the trip home, but I suspect the Army leaders did not want any soldier looking shoddy when he arrived back on U.S. soil.

A legend grew, among the rank and file, about a young soldier who was about to leave Vietnam after serving a year as a combat soldier.

Apparently this young "short timer" was making his final preparations for going home. The soldier's buddies gave him a great send off the day before. One thing led to another and for some reason the soldier failed to get a haircut. When he tried to board the plane the next morning, sure enough he was denied access. He was told to return when his hair was properly trimmed. That evening there was a deadly mortar attack that was directed at the replacement center. This young soldier was killed as he waited for his early morning flight the next day.

I do not know if this story was true, but the soldiers believed it and they had no problem complying with the rules and regulations surrounding departure—especially around haircuts. In addition to these rules, there was a tradition involving the "short timers" worth mentioning. Before you left Vietnam, you were required to find another "short timer." It was your duty to pass your stick and the legend on to the new "short timer" to keep both him and the story alive.

VIETNAM SOUVENIRS

*W*hen people travel they usually like to bring back souvenirs to remind them of their adventures. For soldiers serving their country abroad, the same practice holds true. This is a story about four special souvenirs.

One of my patients was a lieutenant in the Green Beret and he worked with the Montagnards. He would bring in crossbows made by the Montagnards and he gave me three of them. The crossbows he gave me came from three different tribes and they were entirely different from each other. One came from the Rade tribe that was located in the central highlands near the city of Buon Ma Thuot. The second one came from the city of Dalat. The last one came from the area around Pleku. These crossbows are primitive; they are made entirely of wood and vines. They have a hard wood bow, which looked to me like it was made from mahogany. The arrows were made from bamboo and they had a fire-hardened tip. The Montagnards used a type of poison that acted like curare. Fletches of the arrow were made from leaves rather than feathers.

These crossbows became three of my favorite souvenirs from my tour of duty. I obtained a fourth souvenir from a patient whose job it was to collect and dispose of enemy weapons and ordnance. This patient gave me an old battered chi-com carbine. This was a common weapon used by the Viet Cong in the early part of the war. These weapons were hand-me-downs; outdated rifles from the Chinese communists before the North Vietnamese started supplying the VC with the newly manufactured Russian AK-47.

As my tour of duty was concluding, I had my four treasured souvenirs packed and ready to take home. A Vietnamese official told me that I would have no problem bringing home the crossbows, but I would need an export license to bring home a firearm. I asked this official where I could get such a license and he replied "You need to go to Saigon to the national police headquarters in the section called Cho-lon." This request posed a dilemma for me as Saigon was hundreds of miles away and, once in Saigon, I had no idea how to get to Cho-lon.

This dilemma called for some risk-taking. I felt the solution rested with our clerk typist. I asked this typist to type up an official looking document entitled, Certificate of Export. I told him to put all the rubber stamps on it that he could find. Some of these stamps were in English while others were in Vietnamese, and when he was through I had an official looking document.

When it came time to leave Vietnam, I had my crossbows and rifle sticking out of my duffel bag. I boarded the airplane that would take me home; no one questioned me about the rifle. Not one person asked to inspect my "official document." I arrived home safely with my souvenirs, and they are proudly hanging in my home office today.

RETURNING TO THE USA FROM VIETNAM

*M*y Vietnam tour of duty was coming to a close, and two days before my orders would send me to a Replacement Company near Ton Son Nhut airport, some friends threw a party for me at the French restaurant called Forgets. It was a bittersweet time because I was looking forward to going home but I was sad to leave my good friends and the people I had worked with during the past year. With the farewell party behind me, I boarded a C130 transport plane the next morning that would take me to the Replacement Company where I would be processed out of the country.

On the day of departure all personnel who were being sent home were loaded into a truck that would drive them to the airport. I was gratified to see that I was not the only one bringing home war souvenirs. I saw numerous crossbow spears and other weapons sticking out of duffel bags. I didn't feel quite so conspicuous with my chi-com carbine. When the truck arrived at the airport, Army personnel were loaded into a big, shiny blue and white Pan Am jet, although when we got on board, it was obvious that the plane had been modified to carry more personnel than the original luxury liner was built to carry. There was no first or business class section, and there was little leg room.

The first segment of the flight took us from Saigon to Guam. When we landed at Guam, the plane was refueled and we were held up for about half an hour because several B52 bombers were being readied to leave Guam and fly to Vietnam to drop bombs. That was my last contact with the war, and I reminisced about how different it was to be flying away from Guam versus a year earlier when I had stopped in Guam on the troop ship before arriving in Vietnam.

We left Guam and began the long flight back to Travis Air Force Base north of San Francisco. After we landed at Travis, there was a lot of paperwork to be done and the passengers were dispersed to various areas to go on to their new assignments. I was assigned to Letterman General Hospital in the Presidio in San Francisco. I waited to catch a bus that made regular runs to the Oakland Naval Yard, Treasure Island and the Presidio. During this short trip, the bus passed between two hills that came down to the road on both sides. The location of the hills made me feel uneasy because back in Vietnam this would have been a perfect spot for an enemy ambush. I noticed that a few of the other passengers seemed to be uneasy with this geography also. These types of feelings slowly passed but I still feel uneasy if I see an unattended suitcase or bag lying in a public place. When I arrived at the Presidio, the transportation officer told me that my family was waiting for me at an on-base apartment that was kept in the Presidio for families on the move. A jeep was arranged for my transport to reunite me with my family.

Upon arrival at the apartment, my wife, Elizabeth, and my little girl, Christina, who was about five years old, greeted me. Christina was somewhat shy since we had not seen each other since a Hawaiian R & R holiday six months earlier. She quickly warmed up to me, and we became a family once again. We quickly went searching for a place to live and found a comfortable apartment to rent in Tiberon across from the Golden Gate Bridge. I soon began my duties as a staff Neurologist and teacher in a residency program at Letterman General Hospital.

Adjustment to my new routine was difficult and I felt restless. Elizabeth and I had different views of my year in Vietnam. I looked upon the past year as a great learning and life experience. I had both good and bad memories, but I felt that it was an overall positive experience in my life. Elizabeth, on the other hand, felt that it was just a year that we should forget. She viewed it as an entirely negative experience that should be ignored. She wanted to pick up right where we were a year earlier. Our differences in perception were somewhat hard to reconcile, but we did our best at the time. We later divorced.

Moving into a regular work schedule helped me adjust back to my American life. During my war year, I kept personal detailed records of all patients I examined. This discipline later helped me make several presentations about my medical experiences in Vietnam to both army and civilian personnel. I kept in contact over the years with Colonel Carl H. Gunderson, MC USA (Ret.) a professor of Neurology whom I met at the medical field services school in San Antonio Texas and later again at Letterman General Hospital. Dr. Gunderson used my information to publish several articles about my medical experiences in Vietnam.

After the year at Letterman General Hospital, I was discharged from the army and began a 30-year career with the Southern California Permanente Medical Group, which is part of the Kaiser Permanente organization. Upon reflecting about my medical experience in Vietnam and comparing it to my practice at Kaiser Permanente, I gained a couple of insights. While in Vietnam, I saw 22 cases of cerebral malaria, which made me a world expert on that condition. In my 30-year career with Kaiser Permanente, I diagnosed and treated only one case of cerebral malaria, which the patient contracted in Africa. On another occasion, I was asked to consult on a patient at the University of California Irvine who was thought to have cerebral malaria. After examining the patient, I felt the patient did not have this condition, and my diagnosis was confirmed by additional testing. While my vast experience in treating cerebral malaria went largely untapped, some of the other conditions I saw and treated in Vietnam were a great help to me in my medical career. For example, I saw numerous peripheral nerve injuries during the war that were caused by soldiers carrying heavy equipment, sleeping on the ground, and receiving fragment wounds. I was later able to more easily diagnose and treat these conditions in my civilian career because of my war experience.

RETURNING TO VIETNAM ~38 YEARS LATER

*A*s I began writing this collection of short stories about my war experience, I knew that one day I would return to Vietnam. My wife, Roberta, and I made that journey together on October 6, 2004. After a 17-hour flight and a 15-hour time change, I arrived in Vietnam exhausted. I was also quite anxious about stepping back onto Vietnamese soil after 38 years, especially when I saw the name Ton Son Nhut airport. It brought back so many memories. One difference was the name of the city. After the fall of Saigon in 1975, Saigon was renamed Ho Chi Minh City.

As we got off the plane, the temperature and humidity hit us hard. It was only 9:30 in the morning and the temperature was already 86 degrees. I was apprehensive going through customs since all the agents were dressed in army uniforms that had a big red star symbolizing the communist regime, my former enemy.

Roberta and I got through customs easily and, our guide, who had been in the South Vietnamese navy during the war, met us. To make it easy for us, our guide Americanized his name to "Sam." It was easy to find Sam among the hundreds of waiting people at the airport exit area since he held up this sign:

Andy and Roberta Carr
Welcome to Saigon!

Sam quickly navigated us to our van and driver. Over the next ten days, he would slowly introduce us to his beloved country and he shared some personal war experiences with us. As we drove to our Ho Chi Minh City hotel, The Rex, I could not help but notice the changes in the past 38 years. The city seemed familiar, but the people were different. In 1966 most of the women wore *ao dais* which was the national dress for women, and a lot of the men wore military uniforms. Today there was more of a western feel to the dress of both men and women. Only female students now wear the traditional white *ao dais*.

In 1966, the mode of transportation was primarily Pedi cabs and one could find the occasional small motor scooters such as a Vespa. Today the streets are clogged with small motorcycles by the thousands. Sam told us that Ho Chi Minh City has eight million people and three million motorcycles. The motorcyclists have learned to carefully weave in and out of traffic. They wear scarves over their faces to protect them from smog and fumes. The women wear long gloves to protect their skin from the blistering sun. No helmets are required except on the larger highways.

To catch up with jet lag, we napped in our room at the Rex Hotel. At 5:00 P.M. we met Sam who would introduce us to the city and help us secure our first Vietnamese meal. Before dinner we walked through a marketplace that is block upon block of enclosed stalls selling everything from beautiful lacquerware to food delicacies such as dog, snakehead fish, and eels. Getting from one street corner to another was a hazard for us, but not for Sam. The first time I saw a woman cross a busy street, I thought she was either insane or infirm as she walked very slowly across a busy thoroughfare with hundreds of motorcycles passing by. But later, in walking with Sam, I learned the fine art of navigating a busy Ho Chi Minh City street. We learned that to cross a busy street, you walk slowly in a horizontal line so that motorcycles can maneuver around you. At one intersection at least 50 motorcycles passed by us, some as close as inches, but we were never touched. At one point, Roberta just closed her eyes and walked between Sam and me holding both our arms because she was so scared.

For dinner, we asked Sam to take us to a good "locals" place for our first Vietnamese meal. After walking for about an hour and a half, we arrived at a restaurant named *2000*. Sam told us the restaurant got its name following a visit in 2000 by President Clinton who ate at the noodle shop. The restaurant had a casual, open-air environment. It faced a busy street, and it offered plain wooden tables with backless stools in a room full of locals chattering away. The food was plentiful and authentic. We ordered a bowl of rice noodles with chicken, spring rolls and water; it was delicious and quite filling. Roberta and I became reacquainted with chopsticks. The condiments on the table included my old favorite, Nuoc-mam, the unusual smelling fish sauce. President Clinton's picture adorned a wall; the Vietnamese love him because he ate at the restaurant and, more importantly, because he lifted a trade embargo during his Presidency that helped the Vietnamese economy.

The second day of our visit began with breakfast at the Rex Hotel where I enjoyed some fine local cuisine of octopus porridge. Following breakfast, Sam took us out of Ho Chi Minh City toward two destinations: Cao Dai temple in Tay Ninh and to Cu Chi to visit the famous tunnels. Although the trip could have been 25 kilometers, our driver took us on a 65 kilometer scenic path so we could enjoy the beautiful countryside that consisted of rice paddies, rubber plantations, and various other local color.

The Cao Dai temple was a large, spectacular, and somewhat gaudy building. This religion combined Buddha, Confucius, Taoism, and Christianity. Their three divine spiritual deities are Sun Yat-Sen (founder of the Chinese republic), Nguyen Binh Chiem (a great Vietnamese poet), and most surprisingly the French novelist, Victor Hugo. We were able to witness a midday prayer session, which I found interesting because of the costumes, music and ceremony. Cao Dai's followers had sided with the Japanese, then with the French, and then with the U.S during various wars. These people seemed to have an uncanny ability to pick the losers.

The Cu Chi tunnels were of major importance during the Vietnam War. They are a striking testimony to the resourcefulness and determination of the Vietnamese people in the face of the extraordinary military power of America. The Viet Minh built the first tunnels at Cu Chi, 40 kilometers long, in 1948 on a rubber tree plantation, first to hide their arms, and then to hide themselves. From 1960 onwards, the Viet Cong set about repairing and enlarging the network, which finally extended for 250 kilometers. The tunnels were intended to link pockets of resistance fighters and provide backup for hit-and-run attacks on Saigon. The tunnels were three layers deep, and a great deal of fighting took place in and around them. The Americans were desperate to take control of this strategic zone near Saigon and used all possible means to destroy the tunnel network including dropping 500-pound bombs, napalming the area, using flooding and tear gas—all without success. The people of Cu Chi never gave up and America was unable to destroy the tunnels.

When I was in Nha Trang and I heard about the Cu Chi tunnels, I never imagined their extent or complexity. On our tour, a young guide dressed in a Vietnamese military uniform took us to the tunnel entrances, which were so small that the average American could not get in nor traverse them. We got to see some of the chambers where Viet Cong made booby traps from unexploded American bombs, and metal fragments that were collected after bomb raids. We also saw the various methods for making pitfall traps with long metal spikes that were treated with human feces. After seeing the various diabolical devices, I could appreciate some of the major problems we had in treating patients with wounds inflicted by this primitive but effective anti-personnel weapon. At times, wounds did not appear large but they were difficult to treat since they often became infected because of the feces.

As part of our tour, I went down into a tunnel complex that had been enlarged for American tourists, but it still seemed tight and claustrophobic to me. I had to crawl on my hands and knees, whereas our Vietnamese guide could walk in a bent position. The part of the tunnels we visited was about 30 meters long and I was glad to crawl out and see daylight and breathe the fresh air. I do not think I could have handled much more time below the earth. Visiting the tunnels only served to increase my admiration for the Viet Cong who had to endure weeks in these small and crowded tunnels that lacked hygiene and oxygen, had constant dim lights, bad smells, rats, snakes and scorpions. The Viet Cong lived in these atrocious living conditions to avoid the constant bombardment from B52 bombers, napalm, and other warfare tactics. Their survival is a testimony to the strength of the Vietnamese people.

After visiting the tunnels I felt much as a German might feel visiting a holocaust museum. It was a sobering and humbling experience. Everywhere we went the Vietnamese seemed to hold no anger or hostility toward me and I think it is summed up by what our guide Sam told me. "What is past is past and we cannot do anything about it. We look toward the future. We have food to eat, clothes to wear, and I get to make a living doing what I love. What more is there to life?" I wonder how many Americans feel that way?

On my third day in Vietnam, I visited the Reunification Palace (formally known as the Presidential Palace). This palace was the headquarters of the South Vietnamese Presidency up to April 1975 when a tank crashed into the entrance gates marking the end of the war. The palace was then converted into a museum. The upper stories of the palace were devoted to conference rooms where the president conducted interviews and business, and the cabinet held its meetings. There was also a huge banquet room. For me, it was reminiscent of the great castle that the Hapsburgs built outside Vienna because of the way the rooms are laid out—only not on such a grand scale. Located in the lower basement and sub-basement were bunker-like rooms with many maps and communication rooms and even a secret escape tunnel. In one of the map rooms there was a listing of all countries that supplied troops during the war. Viewing this site gave me an eerie feeling as I thought about the current Iraq situation. Once again, the U.S. had the largest number of military personnel leading the war effort. These secret tunnels made me also think of Hitler's last days in Berlin with the underground bunker strategy: Build a bunker in a basement, create your plans, and hunker down out of sight. On the roof of the palace rests a restored Huey helicopter which brought back many memories of me flying down to Cam Ranh Bay or on Medcap missions, which was a medical civilian assistance program.

We left the Reunification Palace and traveled to the War Museum. America calls the war "the Vietnam War" while the Vietnamese call it "the American and their Lackeys Imperialist War." Most of the museum consisted of pictures that were taken to convey the impression of the victories of the North Vietnamese conquering the Americans. I saw the most famous pictures that American photographers took that appeared on the covers of Time, Newsweek, and Life magazines. Our reason for printing the pictures was to show the public the horrors of war. The Vietnamese reason for showing the same pictures was to illustrate war victories. One whole section of the museum was devoted to the 200 war correspondents on both sides who were killed during the war. Another section of the museum was devoted to the "atrocities committed by the Americans against the Vietnamese" during the war. Graphic pictures of beheadings and dismembered children, results of bombing, and several pictures from the My Lai massacre were on display. Of course, there were no pictures of the atrocities performed by the North Vietnamese, which we know happened. There was another section devoted to the alleged effects of Agent Orange, which included a large jar containing a fetus of joined Siamese twins. Another jar contained a markedly deformed fetus. I had already seen similar specimens in a medical pathology museum when I was in medical school, long before Agent Orange was invented. There were pictures of markedly deformed children, which looked to me like examples of osteogenesis imperfecta. When I was seeing patients at the Province hospital in 1966, I saw a child who had a severe case of osteogenesis imperfecta who was born before Agent Orange was ever used.

Another picture that was displayed in the museum was of a man with blisters all over his body, which looked like pemphigitis or as if he was exposed to a blistering agent such as mustard gas. Whether Agent Orange caused all these things is questionable, but the effect of the pictures was quite emotional and they had the intended impact.

The rest of day three was spent visiting the Mekong Delta, which hid Viet Cong and provided rice and other food during the war. Today, life in the Mekong Delta flows to the rhythm of work in the fields and the constant comings and goings of the farmers, on foot, on bicycle, on the backs of buffaloes, by bus, but most of all by boat. Viewing the acres and acres of green rice paddies was a calming sight.

On our fourth day we left Ho Chi Minh City to travel to our next destination, Dalat, a city in the mountainous highland. On our way to Dalat, not far from Ho Chi Minh City, we went through the city of Long Bin, which in 1966 was only a small hamlet and farming area. Today it is a huge industrial area. Long Bin was the town where the American 93rd evacuation hospital was located. During the war I spent ten days at the hospital treating patients. This is the location where I met the actor, John Wayne. The area is now covered with large factories and the nearby airbase of Binh Hoa, where I had landed, is a military air base. The tiny road that I traveled across in fear to get from the airfield to the hospital in 1966 is now a large highway, and the whole area was unrecognizable to me. We only stayed in Long Bin long enough to fill our car tank with gasoline, and buy some drinking water before continuing our journey to Dalat.

On our way to Dalat, we visited a beautiful waterfall, and a Buddhist

Monastery, which was a peaceful, tranquil place with ornate gardens including magnificent aged bonsai. Watching hillside after hillside of lush tea and coffee crops being nourished by gentle rain was a relaxing experience—and quite a contrast from the bustling city of Ho Chi Minh City. I was surprised to see such a robust population in the mountains. When I treated patients from the central highlands in 1966, I was led to believe that few people lived in the highlands. Now I saw houses on either side of the road almost all the way from Ho Chi Minh City to Dalat with many villages along the way. I asked Sam if there was much fighting in the peaceful highlands during the war. "Oh yes!" came his spirited reply. He told me that you could find the Viet Cong within a kilometer along the road we traveled. The city of Dalat—like the city of Nha Trang—saw very little fighting within its boundaries since the Viet Cong used the cities for supplies and R&R until the end of the war.

Dalat is the capital of Lam Dong province and it is about 300 kilometers from Ho Chi Minh City. Dalat provides a breath of fresh air and some wonderful landscapes. Dr. Alexandre Yersin, who was searching this unknown region for a possible area to grow quinquina, discovered Dalat in 1893. The countryside has been extensively developed and the town owes its rich diversity to the indigenous ethnic minorities who live in and around Dalat. Diversity is also seen with fruit and vegetable crops and horticultural activity. A surprise find during our stay in Dalat was embroidery art, a traditional handicraft, which takes an important role in Vietnamese spiritual history. Roberta and I purchased an art piece that depicts springtime. Our picture took the artist about five months to finish because of the detailed silk embroidery design. The art is proudly displayed in our home as a reminder of this trip.

The next morning we left Dalat and on our way to our next destination, Nha Trang, we stopped to visit an eight hundred-year-old Cham temple. The Cham, one of the largest Montagnard tribes, have bequeathed a rich architectural legacy of *kala,* shrine-towers in brick, which can be found dotted along the coast from the Pass of Clouds to Phan Thiet. It is remarkable that these ancient temples are made without mortar. These temples were built in the 13th and 14th centuries and they are still standing today. These monuments show the boundaries of the former kingdom of Champa, which was subsequently absorbed by Vietnam. The Cham originally were Hindu, but later adopted the religion of Islam on contact with Malaysia, whose language is very similar to the Cham language. Still Muslim today, the Cham grow rice and are renowned for their elaborate silk weaving. We met an elderly Cham tribesman who was preparing an offering for a service the next day. In 1968, A Cham tribesman would never have allowed someone to take his picture because of a fear of losing one's spirit. This elderly Cham posed graciously for a photograph, and it is one that I treasure. As I think about America and our need to continuously evolve, I was humbled in the presence of this man whose traditions and life style have not changed much in hundreds of years.

While at the Cham temple, I gazed off into the distance and saw the airstrip in Phan Rang that the Army used in 1966 as a regular stop between Bin Hoa and Nha Trang during the war. Seeing the airstrip brought back vivid memories from my story entitled: The Joy of Being a Commanding Officer. This was the same place where we stopped to pick up a soldier in 1966 who had a chest wound.

After leaving the Cham temple, we headed north around the immense Bay of Cam Ranh. The strategic position of this natural harbor was a temptation that very few major powers were able to resist and it is still home to a military base. Built by the French during the colonial era, it was occupied by the Americans during the Vietnam War and then by the Soviet Union from 1975 to 1990.

Just beyond Cam Ranh, we picked up a superhighway that was recently cut out of the coastal mountains to take us to Nha Trang. As we approached Nha Trang, I found myself filled with anticipation upon returning to the city where I spent the better part of a year. As I entered the city, I saw nothing familiar, and the city appeared to have tripled in size. It was not until I reached the beach that anything seemed familiar. As I looked out to sea, the contour of the beach and the outline of the neighboring islands appeared familiar. Looking back across the beach, I noticed that the city had completely changed. When I was stationed in Nha Trang in 1966, there were French Colonial mansions dotting the main road by the beach. Now there are mostly motels and resorts. While walking down the street, I saw a run down Colonial home with locked gates. I suspected it was waiting its turn to get torn down so a new hotel could be built. The airfield had been the center of our world, with its constant flow of medevac helicopters, C123 and C130 troop transport planes, and large starlifter jets evacuating patients back to the States. It is still there, but it is off limits for civilians so I could not tour the area. "Tent City" is now a hugely developed business and housing center, and the beach where I first landed and struggled in the sand is now an exclusive resort surrounded by palm trees and lush vegetation. I could not locate Beach house #1, but there are some fancier restaurants scattered along the beach.

One evening, Roberta and I met an old, sun-aged woman selling necklaces and prawns on the beach—an interesting combination. We engaged her to prepare the prawns for our dinner. She used her private hibachi that was set-up on the public beach next door to an airy outdoor restaurant where we sat down. We ordered two Tiger beers, fried rice and salad to accompany the prawns and enjoyed the meal on a warm, balmy Vietnamese evening. If I closed my eyes, I could almost transport myself back 38 years. Our cook tried to sell us necklaces for dessert, but we passed.

In my quest to find something familiar, I looked at a map of Nha Trang and saw that the local province hospital where I had conducted a clinic once a week to treat Vietnamese patients was still in the same place it had been on Yersin Street. I asked Sam to drive me to the hospital and when I arrived, I saw a modern, seven-story building. I told Sam that was not the facility I was looking for and he guided me through the hospital onto the grounds behind it. There, in an extremely run down condition, is where I found the province hospital that I remembered. Next to it was the pediatric building where I frequently saw patients, and it was in a dilapidated condition. In fact, the building looked as if it was in the process of being torn down. The old hospital building was open so we meandered over to it to have a look. I remembered the operating room as well as some of the patient rooms and the treatment room where I conducted my clinic. The rooms were now being used for storage. It was a bittersweet memory: bitter in the sense of seeing the hospital I remember with such fond memories being in such disrepair, and sweet in the sense that a brand new modern hospital was available for patients. Of interest, while Vietnam describes itself as a socialistic nation, health care is not available to anyone without money. The exception is for government employees and then it is only for the employee—not for the employee's family. Sam told me that the average person goes without health care, finds remedies through family contacts, or saves money to see a qualified physician. Most go without basic health care services.

Following our visit to the province hospital, I tried to find the location of both the 8th Field Hospital where I worked and the villa where I lived during the war. The area is located adjacent to the airport, which is now a military instillation, and I was disappointed that civilians were not allowed access to the area.

We traveled north of Nha Trang looking for the Korean hospital that I visited during the war. I recognized the hill that I climbed while walking through the minefield; I closed my eyes and imagined how I felt when the helicopter picked me up from the top of it. The land where the Korean hospital was built is now only a lush green valley. Someone not associated with the war would have no idea of the soldiers whose lives were saved by the physicians caring for him or her on this hallowed ground.

On the way back to town, we passed the road to the missionaries' home that I described earlier in this book. An exclusive resort is now built on the land that was home to that wonderful family with whom I shared a Christmas so many years ago.

There was one last place Sam wanted to take me before the tour day ended. He drove us to a large hotel resort complex across the street from the ocean, and we took the elevator up to the 20th floor. Upon exiting the elevator I immediately knew why Sam selected this place for me. I beheld an amazing 360 panoramic view of Nha Trang from an observation deck high above the city. As I looked around, I could appreciate how much the city had changed—and stayed the same. New buildings were all around me; yet the hills and mountains surrounding Nha Trang, and the ocean and islands were all the same. Standing there and looking out, I felt as if I was coming back from a Medcap mission in a Huey helicopter just before landing at the heliport next to the hospital. I took a deep breath and released both air and the hold this place has had on me for the past 38 years.

After breakfast the next morning, we headed toward our next and last stop in Vietnam, Mui Ne, a quiet fishing village that is famous for the astonishing sight of its exceptional high dunes of orange-colored sand overlooking the sea. I had not visited this place during the war, nor was I particularly interested in visiting it now. Sam asked us to trust his recommendation to end our Vietnam adventure at Mui Ne. The village stands on a picturesque bay bathed by the turquoise waters of the South China Sea, which break against a long white sandy beach. Sam booked us into a brand new hotel and we were probably one of ten families staying in the beautiful sprawling hotel, Pandanus Beach Resort. Soon after we checked in, Roberta and I changed into our bathing suits, grabbed our water bottles and books, and claimed two-cushioned lounge chairs under a thatched umbrella nestled in a small cove along the beach. We barely moved for a day and a half. We read our books, drank our water and Roberta enjoyed a spa treatment that cost $10 for 90 minutes. We enjoyed a swim in both the ocean and fancy pool, and we basked in the quietness of this little piece of heaven on earth. We took Sam and our driver out to dinner on our last evening to a local's restaurant right by the beach. We wanted to thank our new friends for their kindness and planning that made this trip so memorable.

On our way to the airport the next day, I stopped in Phan Thiet to purchase some Nuoc-mam, my delicious fish sauce, to take back home. Unlike in 1966 when I was afraid to pack it, I took a risk this time. I crossed my fingers and hoped that none of the liquid would escape from its glass container (it made the trip just fine). We traveled through Ho Chi Minh City/Saigon one last time. I don't know what I truly expected to feel after spending time in post-war Vietnam, but I did experience calmness about returning to the place of so much controversy, violence, and life-altering experiences. I did find closure on this part of my life that has been kept alive for so many years.

OUR VIETNAMESE GUIDE, "SAM"

*W*hen I set out to write this book, I had no intention of writing a chapter about our guide. After spending ten days with Sam, I need to tell a little of his story because it was really part of my story too.

Using the Internet, Roberta found Sam, who would become our personal guide for a 10-day customized tour. Not being part of a formal tour group made us both a bit nervous. References from prior Australian and English customers gave us the confidence to hire Sam, and both Roberta and I were deeply moved by our time with him. Over the ten days, Sam shared many personal stories. On our last evening, I told him about my book and he gave me permission to tell some of his stories. Sam asked me not to use his real name for fear of government retaliation.

Sam is a survivor on so many levels. I believe his stories will give you an idea of the strength of the Vietnamese people as a whole. Before Roberta and I left America, Sam sent us an email asking for a favor. He asked us to buy a radar detector for him, and he told us he would pay us back in Vietnam. We learned that the radar detector technology was not available in Vietnam, and this piece of technology was important to his job. Sam described the police corruption that exists today in Vietnam. I read Nelson DeMille's book *Up Country* about Vietnam and I thought DeMille exaggerated the police corruption situation a little. DeMille was quite accurate. In Vietnam if you are caught speeding, you receive a fine and you get a hole punched in your driver's license by the policeman. If you are caught speeding a second time, the fine is higher and a second hole is punched in your license. For a third violation you receive a third hole, and your driver's license is taken away. If you are a tour director, your livelihood is also taken away from you. The tickets can be easily avoided by paying an expensive bribe to the police officer. With this in mind, one can see how a radar detector would be a prized possession for our guide and his driver who spend their lives navigating the highways.

When we first met, Sam told me he was especially happy to be our guide because he and I were both veterans of the war and we both fought on the same side. He was in the South Vietnamese Navy. He learned his English in high school and he perfected it on an assignment to San Diego, California where he became proficient in deciphering codes. His main job in the Navy was in breaking and translating North Vietnamese coded messages, and in translating and sending coded messages for the South Vietnamese and American military leaders.

Sam crossed paths with Senator John Kerry. The U.S. Presidential election was a little more then two weeks away and Sam told us that during the war he was stationed in the delta area for a few months and he met and worked with Kerry. He liked Kerry and hoped he would win the election. Sam traveled to Nha Trang where he attended the naval academy. While Sam arrived after I left Nha Trang, he felt a kinship with me because of my year spent in the city. Sam has a great affinity for the Americans with whom he served.

Sam barely escaped from Nha Trang in 1975, just two weeks before the fall of Saigon. Many of his friends and fellow sailors were killed trying to make it to the last ship to leave Nha Trang harbor. He told me that he literally had to step over bodies to board the ship, which was under constant fire. The ship sailed to Saigon and it soon left for open sea to escape the North Vietnamese invasion. Sam, however, could not leave his family or his beloved country behind, and he disembarked from the ship. He was quickly arrested upon his return to Saigon, and he and his family were forced to leave their home on twelve hours' notice. They could take only the clothes on their back and small bags of family belongings with them.

Sam was sent to a prisoner of war or "rehabilitation" camp and forced to do hard labor in the mountains. Food consisted of measly portions of dirty white rice, and Sam had constant "reeducation" lessons. Disease and despair were part of everyday life. He told me that many people died under these horrible conditions. Sam told me that he pretended to be "reeducated," so he was released from the camp after four grueling years. He said other prisoners spent many more years in camp because they refused to be "reeducated." While in camp, Sam had a few trusted friends with whom he practiced speaking English. He told us that even under these harsh camp conditions, he knew he would be released one day and that speaking English would be the key to his future. He and his friends would whisper together during the late night, and they were careful not to get caught to avoid being severely punished for this transgression.

After being released from the camp, Sam spent several months trying to find his family. He soon learned that anyone associated with being a South Vietnamese sympathizer was not allowed to remain in Saigon. He found his destitute family near the Cambodian border. Sam worked at many small jobs to earn enough money to simply feed his family. For example, he planted rice and other crops for the government, and he drove a Pedi cab for pennies. He said he had a hard time until 1988 when the communist government relaxed many of its stringent rules and allowed farmers to grow their own rice for the first time. Although jobs were starting to open for the former South Vietnamese military soldiers in Ho Chi Minh City, discrimination was clearly present. For example, Sam was not legally allowed to become a tour guide, live in Saigon, or hold a government job. Sam obtained a tour guide license only after he saved enough money to bribe an official to issue the license. He has to renew his license every six months, which is costly for him.

Sam described two other factors that are changing the landscape: property ownership and commerce. To this day, the government owns all the land in Vietnam, but now the Vietnamese can purchase long-term land leases. Sam was never able to purchase a long-term lease for his home because of his military background, but he was able to strike a deal to purchase his home through a relative. There is high trust and a strong bond between family members in Vietnam. When President Clinton lifted the trade embargo in 1992, the government started to become more interested in commerce than on monitoring people in Sam's situation. High tech companies are starting to spring up throughout the country.

Sam shared a poignant story involving his son, "Jon" and grandson, "Billy" that illustrates the prejudice he and his family faced. Jon fell in love and married the daughter of a North Vietnamese official. Upon Billy's birth, the girl's parents kept him in their home, and they would not let Jon see the infant. One night, while he was riding his motorcycle on his way to try to see the child, Jon was killed in an auto accident. Soon after the funeral, Sam's daughter-in-law asked Sam to raise Billy. While Billy still lives with Sam today, his former daughter-in-law married an American and moved to the United States several years ago. Now that she is out of the clutches of her family, she wants to regain custody of Billy whom she never stopped loving. She and Sam are in the process of working this arrangement out. Sam would love to keep his grandson with him, but he feels that Billy would have a better life and more opportunities in America than he could have in present day Vietnam.

I asked Sam if he would ever like to live in America. Legally he can never leave Vietnam because of his military background, but officials can, of course, be bribed. Sam told me some of these stories through tears, others through angry, frustrated emotional outbursts. One thing is certain. Despite everything he has been though, he genuinely loves his country and he would never consider leaving it. He would rather stay in Vietnam and work to rebuild it and leave a legacy for his family.

EPILOGUE: THE "WHAT IFS"

*A*fter writing this book and spending ten days in Vietnam, I could not help but think about some of the "what ifs" one ponders after undergoing such a life-changing experience.

What if...the U.S. had "won" the war? Would Vietnam be better off than it is now? Would the people be better off? Would democracy have taken place? Vietnam had a democracy before the U.S. involvement, but there was so much corruption that it did not work. The Vietnamese had been fighting for their independence for a thousand years. Would they have stopped just because America had won the war? I don't think so. It is my belief that America would have needed to maintain troops for years afterwards to keep the factions from fighting much as we're doing in Iraq today. I do not think we would have ever won the war.

What if...Ho Chi Minh had lived beyond 1967? Would his type of communism be seen in the country now? Certainly the people seem to revere Ho Chi Minh—even those who fought for South Vietnam. The South Vietnamese just did not like Ho Chi Minh's type of communism; they knew about the atrocities that he committed to maintain discipline around his own ideology. But from what I have read about Minh, and after listening to what several Vietnamese have told me about him, I think that his form of communism was more people oriented and the people of Vietnam would be better off today if he had lived.

What if...we had never gotten into the Vietnam War in the first place? My guess is that the North would have taken over the entire country much sooner, the loss of life would have been much less, and probably the form of government would be much the same as it is today. I find myself wondering if the loss of 58,000 Americans and an estimated two million Vietnamese was for nothing. Additionally, I suspect that the U.S. government would have recognized the Vietnamese government as a fair trading partner, sooner and Vietnam would be further along on its way toward being an accepted nation in the world.

A quote from Aldous Huxley summarizes a philosophy about history that I have come to embrace. "That men do not learn very much from the lessons of history is the most important of all the lessons that history has to teach." That is a quote worth remembering as we navigate the world conflicts today.

ISBN 1-41205718-3